THE REBELLIOUS WIDOW

A PRACTICAL GUIDE TO LOVE AND LIFE
AFTER LOSS

JILL JOHNSON-YOUNG

Printed in the United States of America

First Printing, 2020

Ebook ISBN 978-0-578-82045-3

Softcover ISBN 978-0-578-82044-6

Discounts are available for bulk quantities for academic or clinical
purposes. For information on bulk discounts or booking Jill for your
next event, please email admin@jilljohnsonyoung.com.

Cover photo credit: Nicole Anderson www.nicolebranderson.com

Cover design credit: Adam Davis

CONTENTS

Dedication   v
Introduction   xi
Foreword   xxv

1. Adjusting to Your Loved One's   1
   Terminal Diagnosis
2. Helping Your Loved One Cope with   21
   Their Own Grief
3. Your New Role as a Caregiver   33
4. Maximize the Time You Have Left   47
   Together
5. Hospice Care 101   59
6. Saying Goodbye   74
7. Rewriting the Grief Paradigm   94
8. Buck the Rules   111
9. Prepare for Change   124
10. Envision a New Life   140
11. Live Your Life and Find Love Again   162
12. A Life on Your Own Terms   177

Additional Information   187
Acknowledgements   189
Notes   193

DEDICATION

I have had the intimate experience of having walked two beloved women who loved me without reservation out of this world. Through my lives with Linda Johnson-Young (1952-2010) and Kathy Casper (1955-2013) I learned what it means to love, grieve, reorganize and to once again find the sunshine, smiles and joy that are supposed to be in life. And so first and foremost, this book is dedicated to their memories, and the smiles they will always bring to those who loved them. (And my smile as I remember the occasional naughtiness we created).

This dedication goes also to my third wife, Hannah Stacie Reedy, who helped me with both of their deaths, and challenged me to create a way to finish my grief. To construct living memories without making my life about being widowed, and take them with me into my new life and plans. I am blessed to be sharing this new chapter with a kind and loving spouse who was brave enough to marry someone who was widowed twice before reaching fifty. (I mean really- can you imagine telling anyone you are doing that?). Fortunately, as the funeral director she could say with confidence she knew the causes of death, and that I was not brewing oleander soup for dinner.

Finally, my children Kerry, Charity, and Chloe deserve a shout out. From landing in a two-mom home out of foster care as older kiddos, to losing mama, welcoming and then losing their stepmom, and for adapting to one change after another- I am so glad you are mine, and proud of each of you. Thanks for supporting this mom in recreating my life and career. Katrina, our extra child who is now stuck with us as the moms still here, I owe you forever and I am so glad you are ours as well as your mom's. All of you were, and are, amazing. Together we are the family that knows how to celebrate life and get through the losses. (And go to Hawaii for shave ice). (In our family we go out for ice cream after someone dies, and then to Hawaii when I can herd them onto a plane)

My hope is that this book will take each reader through their own goodbye and into a happy and successful recovery, with the memory of their spouse tucked in with them along the way.

PRAISE FOR JILL JOHNSON-YOUNG

Jill Johnson-Young's *The Rebellious Widow* combines professional wisdom and practical guidance with her own personal story and journey with the hospice process and loss of loved ones. It addresses the challenges of holding onto hope, and courage through loss and life as it passes while we struggle through trying to keep going with the daily demands of life, relationships and roles. This story provides an incredible guide through something none of us ever want to experience, let alone think about, offering grounding and a way to recreate that new normal that was never asked for or wanted. Heartfelt and powerful guidance that is tried and true, it gives permission to love, remember, move forward and create growth as one's life continues forward. This very personal story tells all of the challenges faced after very difficult grief processes, not once, but twice; and how love and grief can co-exist as the survivors create a rich journey that is cumulative in time, carrying the best of the past experiences, and integrating and building a strong present, for a solid foundation for the future. I especially enjoyed the idea of rebelling against ideas and roles that aren't necessarily helpful to anyone who is grieving and trying to create some sense of normalcy and identity under very difficult circumstances. Rebellion in service of healing, redefining ones' self and personal growth? You bet! And, with dignity, honest communication, and hopefulness is the best respect we can pay ourselves and our loved ones. I highly recommend this read, and it will have a home on the lending library in my office for those who may need it.

-K. R. Juzwin, PsyD, Licensed Clinical Psychologist, Illinois, Professional Certification in Police Psychology, Diplomate #67, Society for Police & Criminal Psychology

Jill Johnson Young empowers spouses/ partners with knowledge of the death and dying western culture and gives permission to break ties with outdated and emotionally hurtful societal customs and 'norms.' Jill states the importance of therapeutic humor within the death and dying process, understanding that many will not agree with humor at such a 'solemn' time. Jill understands that humor and shared laughter encourages the last remaining moments of emotional intimacy between partners and their family. In turn, poignant memories of the deceased are created that allow the bereaved to breathe in with an AH and out with a HA. Thank You for writing this book.

- Rev Debra Joy Hart RN, Certified Humor Professional, Grief Support Counselor., Author: Grandma D's Bubbles

As a widow, I wish I had this book 3 years ago when my partner was first diagnosed with cancer. The wisdom in this book will help support and empower you during a very unsettling and challenging time. If you are facing the possibility of losing your partner or have lost a loved one, I highly recommend, "The Rebellious Widow: Reclaiming life and love after loss".

- *Liz Acar, LCSW, Empowerment Specialist, Motivational Speaker, 3 time #1 Best-Selling Author, and Publisher Photographer. www.Liz-Acar.com*

This is the book I wish I had when my boyfriend Mark passed away from cancer in 2015. Jill's experience of the loss of a spouse (two!) and her work with end-of-life patients and their families infuse this book with authenticity and accuracy. Her recommendations on self-care, especially doing grief your own way, will help anyone in a relationship with a terminal patient or who just lost their person.

- *Becky Whatley, Riverside CA*

INTRODUCTION

Life is not what it's supposed to be. It's what it is. The way you cope with it is what makes the difference.

-Virginia Satir

The Moment the World Stopped

My wife Linda and I had been together for twenty years and were raising two teenage daughters when we received some of the worst news any couple will ever hear in their lifetimes: her sudden frequent bouts of what we had believed to be pneumonia were actually symptoms of advanced pulmonary fibrosis (PF). A breast cancer survivor, the chemo that had saved Linda's life eight years prior had damaged her lung tissue beyond repair.

This time, no matter how courageously she

fought, how much she exercised, or how hard we prayed, and bargained, and tried, it was clear that PF would win the battle. We had to get ready. We had to get the kids ready.

Mama was going to die.

The afternoon we realized what was coming, we stopped for a glass of expensive cabernet at the Mission Inn, our favorite spot to celebrate. In years past, sitting at this same table—*our* table—under a window in the hotel lobby, we'd toasted her retirement, our anniversaries, and our wedding. We'd even taken our daughter Kerry there for her prom.

There we sat sipping our wine, reminiscing. We texted the kids that we would be home later. Intuiting what was really going on, Kerry replied, "This is it, isn't it, Mom? Mama's really dying now."

Our hearts broke reading her words. There was no protecting ourselves or our girls from Linda's approaching death. No stopping or hiding from it. This was *really* happening. To us, Jill and Linda. Someday not too far off, I would just be Jill again.

What would that even mean anymore, after decades of being half of a loving, committed couple who'd built a life together?

I was about to find out.

The Rules

As it turns out, what life as a widow was *supposed* to look like had already been decided for me. There were societal rules for this, I learned. A lot of them.

And woe to the widow who steps one foot out of line
—for she will hear about it from damn near everyone
—friends, family, acquaintances, and even strangers.

I was lucky in that I had some forewarning about
this. Soon after Linda died, a friend who'd previously
lost her wife met me at Starbucks to impart a lesson
she said she'd wished someone had told her: society's
many, *many* expectations of widows. It's worth noting
that these rules are different for women than for
men. And since I'm writing about my own experiences in this book, the focus will be primarily on the
rules as they apply to us ladies. But guys, if you're
reading, a good deal of this will apply to your experiences too, if you're a widower or will soon
become one.

Here are the highlights of the rules of being a
widow, especially if you live in a town where every-
body knows your name:

- Do not be seen smiling
- Best to look sad—but not too sad, so you
  don't make others sad or uncomfortable
- No going out for anything social
- No bright- or light-colored clothing
  allowed; only black
- NO DATING
- Make no changes to your house involving
  your lost loved one until given permission
  (by whom exactly is unclear)
- Get your spouse's stuff out of the house
  right away so it doesn't upset people

- Don't say their name
- Do say their name, but apologize for it because you are making others uncomfortable
- Be prepared to be criticized for your behavior, by anyone, at any time, no matter what you do . . . or don't do
- These rules are in effect for as long as the person admonishing you for breaking them thinks is appropriate

Hearing my friend's words as she broke this down for me made my head spin. I was the one who was widowed. Wasn't it *my* decision what to do with my life?

As she was kind enough to warn me, the answer was a resounding "no" from many corners. And never mind that half of these rules directly contradict each other either. Whether I liked it or not, they all applied to me now, as they apply to *all* widows.

I have had complete strangers tell me in the grocery line that if they were widowed, they would never date again. "It would be wrong," a church friend who'd lost her dad told me, in front of my second wife and my kids, adding that if her mom ever dated again she would "never forgive her." I lost a close friend after she cussed me out upon learning I planned to remarry after my first wife's death. Even my daughter's *therapist* told me, after learning I was dating as a widow, that if he died, he would not want another man "riding my bike or my wife."

It never ceases to amaze me that people who are uncomfortable with death and who have never lost a spouse themselves could presume to know what is right for someone who *has* been widowed—in my case, not once, but *twice*. And yet it happens. A lot.

If you are already widowed, chances are you have stories like this of your own to tell. And if you've only recently learned you'll be joining this club, believe me when I tell you: you will have stories to tell about this one day too.

But does that mean we're doomed to sitting at home for endless months or years, doing nothing but wearing black mantillas and draping the furniture with black crepe in order to convince some folks we're grieving enough to meet *their* needs and expectations?

I'm here to tell you, definitively: *hell no*. But first you have to be prepared to tell people—as politely and graciously—or not, as you please—where they can stick all those nonsensical and cruel rules.

You prepared as best you could for this loss. You're knee-deep now in managing your grief and getting back to the daily business of managing your life. On top of all of this, if you want to get through this difficult period in one piece and find the happiness you deserve on the other side of it?

There's one more thing you have to be . . .

The Rebellious Widow

Being a rebellious widow means seizing control of your own destiny rather than letting others dictate it for you based on a bunch of external, nonsensical rules. You get to make your own rules, set your own expectations. You get to decide what path you want to follow.

A rebellious widow must also develop the resilience needed to let the insensitive and even cruel things people will say roll off your back. Even the most well-meaning people in your life may question your decisions. They may ask *how dare you* find the courage and strength to reimagine your life, to keep living it rather than to feel and behave indefinitely as though you had died too.

You'll learn a little more about me below, but it's important to know here that I'm a therapist who specializes in grief counseling. In my many years of teaching people how to cope with death, dying, grief, and loss, I've learned an important lesson that research is just now catching up to: Widows who expect the death of their spouse due to a terminal diagnosis and walk through this process as a caregiver tend to process and heal through their own grief far sooner than the other people around them.

Why? Because we are right in the thick of it. We *have* to get ready. Like it or not, death is coming. So, we grieve early and often. We plan and prepare. We reorganize a new life for ourselves in our mind as a means of coping.

We do this because we have to know we are going to survive. We have to be able to tell our spouses goodbye and assure them it's okay for them to go. Those not thrust into this awful role tend to hold out hope even where there is none. It's easy when you're not the one who vowed to be there every day to not see the advance of the illness, or to leave when things get too hard. The other people in your life don't have to reorganize to cope, because when that death occurs, their lives will not change all that much. Yes, they will miss someone they loved too, but not in the same way. And they usually don't start grieving until the person they love is gone. So they finish grieving far behind the widow—and they tend to have a hard time understanding that the widow has already done a great deal of her grieving before that death ever occurred.

The other reality is that most people have all sorts of deep-seated fear and discomfort when it comes to the topics of death, dying, loss, and our own mortality. We all have to work through these issues in our own time, but that doesn't give us the right to project that baggage onto other people—especially those who have suffered a major loss like the death of a spouse. This fear is the other half of what lies at the root of 'the Rules' I outlined in the section above.

If you choose to live your life according to these rules, make no mistake: you're letting fear and other people's expectations dictate your life and your happiness. That's not what you want for yourself. It's certainly not what your spouse would want for you.

Being a rebellious widow means learning to recognize this truth at the heart of 'the Rules.' It means creating healthy boundaries to protect ourselves from those who can't or *won't* see it. And you may be surprised by who is still standing by you when you come out on the other side. Sometimes those closest to us are those who feel the most strongly that *they get a say* in how we should grieve. They are sorely mistaken.

You must develop the ability to keep your eyes focused on where you need and want to go—not in a *selfish* way, but simply enough to do what is needed to take care of yourself. You can't allow yourself to be distracted or dragged down by other peoples' opinions about what you decide you need to be okay as you move forward. Your ability to master this new mindset is what will set the tone for the rest of your life.

The task of the rebellious widow is nothing short of this: to create your own new life. You are not leaving your spouse behind. They mattered when they were alive, and they matter now. You will always talk to them, consult them, remember them. Your new life will include them.

But it has to be *yours* now.

To get there, you'll need a plan and a support system. We'll cover how to nail down these two key elements in the chapters to come.

From One Rebellious Widow to Another

So, you might wonder: who is this Jill lady and what does *she* know about grieving? The simple answer is this: more than I ever expected to, even as a former hospice worker and a therapist who specializes in grief and loss.

I am a Licensed Clinical Social Worker (LCSW) and the co-owner and CEO of Central Counseling Services, where I see clients and run the clinical side of our psychotherapy practice. Over the last ten years, we've grown from just two of us to a staff of twenty-eight therapists working out of two offices and in one local school, with more locations in the planning stages. We include a wide variety of specializations including my own in dementia and grief and loss. We also have a teaching facility in our main office where we train therapists and other professionals, and I speak on the national circuit to other industry professionals about death and dying. My message focuses on how to address death and loss in a way that offers hope and recovery from grief. I've also established an online grief program, Your Path Through Grief, with an intensive focus on the first year after a major loss.

Before opening our practice, I spent more than a decade in hospice work in two states—first as a social worker, and later as a director in charge of a large team of social workers, bereavement center staff, and chaplains. I had the good fortune to be part of opening a residential hospice wing where our patients could come with their families and remain together until the patient's death. In Florida I also ran children's grief programs in the local schools and for adults in community settings. It was a combination of all these professional experiences that shaped me into the therapist I am today.

I have published three books about grief for children (*Someone is Sick: How Do I Say Goodbye?*, *Someone I Love Just Died: What Happens Now?* and *My Pet Is Sick: It's Time to Say Goodbye*). These works have been well-received by parents, funeral directors, faith communities, and young readers. I also authored a grief workbook, *Your Own Path through Grief: A Workbook for Your Journey to Recovery*. I've received awards for my work as a social worker in both Florida and California, and have also presented at state conferences for California Funeral Directors, the National Association of Social Workers, and the California Association of Marriage and Family Therapists. I've spoken at national conferences—including one for SAMHSA—and internationally. I also speak frequently for local groups across the country, including keynoting and facilitating speaker's panels, and have been featured on a number of podcasts for grief and loss, and for therapists grappling with these issues both personally and professionally.

In my personal life, I've adopted three wonderful children, two with my first wife, and one after her death. I have been married three times, and as I mentioned earlier here, I've been widowed twice. I lost Linda, my wife of twenty-three years in 2010.

And after I found love again—to my chagrin, with the very person my stubborn Linda picked out for me while she was dying— I lost my second wife, Casper, a few years later.

I know all too intimately the pain of losing the person you've built a life with and around. That doesn't mean I know exactly what it's like or will be like for you, but I've walked down this road enough to become an expert on navigating its dangers and pitfalls. I've also had the benefit of my professional training to help me steer myself through it all. Even so, I wish I'd had someone to teach me the things I'm going to teach you here, dear reader. So much so that I knew I had to write this book.

How to Get the Most Out of This Book

This book was born out of a series of blogs I wrote as my first two wives—first Linda, and then a few years later, Casper—were sick and dying. Originally, I was writing because it helped me to keep friends and family informed about what was happening and to process my own grief. This time around, my aim is to help you process yours.

The Rebellious Widow is designed to prepare you for the loss of your spouse, and for what comes after. In learning what I have to teach here, born from my own professional and personal experiences, you'll know what to expect not just after your spouse has died, but before and during too. Armed with this knowledge, you'll be able to plot the course for your own recovery in whatever way works best for you.

The first half of the book covers what happens before and during your spouse's death, from the day you get the awful news of a terminal diagnosis, to your loved one's final moments. In the second half, I cover what happens next, starting with how to take care of yourself in those first few awful weeks and months of loss, all the way through how to boldly go forth and seize every bit of the joy this world still holds for you.

Regardless of where you're at in the grieving process, my recommendation is to read the book from start to finish, marking it up as you go to note any sections that you find particularly helpful or that resonate for you. Even if you've already been widowed, you may find that the information I share in the first half to be affirming, or that it helps you to resolve some lingering trauma that may have resulted from lack of access to education about the death process. If you are soon to be widowed, you'll want to read not just the first half, but also the second so that you know what lies ahead and how best to prepare yourself.

Once you've finished your first read-through, you'll always be able to come back as needed to refresh yourself on useful strategies or proactive suggestions for wherever you find yourself along the way.

My Promise to You

I can't and won't make promises about how long

your journey through grief will take. I can promise, though, that you will be happier and healthier if you embrace the path of the Rebellious Widow than you would be trying to abide by other people's rules.

Grievers who laugh, smile, and get some sun are the healthy ones, the ones who survive. Some consider it a romantic ideal for a person who has just lost their spouse to die shortly afterward. The reality is that this is a thing that can and does *really happen*—because some people either lose the will to live when their loved one goes first, or they've done so poor a job of taking care of their own health that they too wind up falling gravely ill. Believe it or not, grief can cause a heart attack in the initial moments or hours after a spouse dies. Later on it causes inflammation, which means someone not ready for what's coming can succumb to a heart attack or stroke. If you are reading this, then at least some part of you wants to survive this, to have a new life on the other side of grief.

This is absolutely possible. All you have to do to start yourself on this path is to decide to walk it.

I don't follow rules well. I especially do not follow the Widow Rules well. We don't get along even a little bit. I've lived an unconventional life, so I see no reason to do widowhood any differently. And I've never been sorry I chose the path of the Rebellious Widow.

You will never stop loving your spouse or honoring their memory. Even so, their death does not mean you can't ever be happy again, or can't love someone else. Remember, this is your loss. Your path. Your recovery. Yours to make of it what you will.

Remember too that every time we make a widow into a rebel, we help the next one after her.

So here is to you, dear reader, a Rebellious Widow in the making.

FOREWORD

When I met Jill I was stuck in the grief of losing my Mum in a tragic motor vehicle accident. I did not know I was stuck. I thought I was living on the edge of major depression so I 'dug deep', put on a smiling face, and got on with my life, keeping in the periphery the overwhelming pain of my mother's death

I didn't want to be depressed but we were 5 years after death so I shouldn't be still grieving right? Afterall don't the rules tell us that if we go through the stages of grief then we will get through the grieving period and then we will have completed our grieving and then someone we enter into a post grief life where...Ummm well I don't know what I was expecting, possibly not to hurt when I thought about my Mum anymore.

Jill talks about the Rules that were thrust upon her as she became a widow for the first time. It is also my experience that we have rules about grief, about death, and about dying. We as humans like these rules, they comfort us to know there will be an end to the pain.

However, my pain didn't seem to be ending despite following the rules and acknowledging the stages (which aren't helpful if we are honest they just leave us feeling like we are failing at grief). Jill gave me some advice that was almost a throwaway comment – *Jo, you can honour and remember your Mum anyway you want to. There are no rules.*

Reading those words now I go, well of course. That is so simple. But in 2015 when I was still so incredibly raw and scared of the emotional pain, these words were a breath of fresh air. What if I could do this thing called grief in the way that worked for me?

I witnessed my family stuck in their grief too, my grandmother, my son, my father my sisters, my uncles. People would speak about Mum and then start to tear up and then express how sorry they were for tearing up and then be ashamed that they were still hurting. So essentially what had happened is that someone we loved so very much became a source of shame. That can't be a healthy stage of grief?

With Jill's help, I started creating words, and ways of asking questions about my Mum to stimulate conversations to bring who she was to the front of mind and allow people the opportunity to talk about her, remember her, experience her again. And you know what – in this act of rebellion we saw a remarkable transformation. Dying and death became just a little bit easier to talk about, and we started living a life that included Mum again.

This was extremely helpful because 10 years after my Mum was killed in a motor vehicle accident, my Dad was killed in a workplace accident.

This second experience was hard. But it was different. I was different and I had thrown away the rule book, and stopped fearing my pain and anger, and stopped fearing that I was going to become clinically depressed.

During this time Jill never said to me

- You know what to do
- You've got this
- You've been through this before, so it will be easier this time

No Jill said –

Oh Jo this just sux

Oh your poor family this must hurt so much

These words were kind and brought so much relief to an incredibly painful situation. It also acknowledged the truth, this was painful, this was a unique situation and nothing about this was going to be painless. While mourning my father was difficult, I didn't have the same experience of shame that I had with Mum.

In 2020 I was diagnosed with breast cancer. The treatment has been rough and presented so many opportunities for me to grieve. Grieve the potential loss of my future, grieve the loss of my hair, the loss of my independence, the loss of my function, and the loss of parts of my own body with a double amputation.

Again Jill has been unwavering in her ability to read me, sending me sometimes hilarious cards, and sometimes thoughtful and beautiful cards, sending me must do's like – please go and play with your puppy now, and asking me to write this foreword.

I've also had the honour to watch Jill grow into her own as a speaker, author, and trainer. She is not scared of talking about dying, death, and grief, and as weird as it might be to read this statement, she is an expert in this topic both as a licensed clinical social worker and as a 2x widow. Jill is evidenced-based practice plus lived experience. Every time she presents people thank her for the way she informs, imparts, and makes sense of topics we are generally scared of.

Dying, death and grief are not going away any time soon. So why not learn how to integrate these experiences into our lives? This practice of integration allows me to honour my parents because I am not scared to talk about them, to speak to their flaws, and their wonderfulness. It enables me to feel my feelings knowing they are real, they are right, and I am OK. In short, knowing my grief and how to grieve empowers me to heal.

Thank you Jill for the Rebellious Widow. Thank you for making something unspeakable to be something worth valuing.

Jo Muirhead

> *Daughter*
> Consultant Rehabilitation Counsellor
> Founder Purple Co PL
> Author *The Entrepreneurial Clinician*
> Creator of *The Book of Evidence*
> www.purpleco.com.au
> www.jomuirhead.com

ADJUSTING TO YOUR LOVED ONE'S TERMINAL DIAGNOSIS

> The most painful thing to experience is not defeat but regret.

> — Leo Buscaglia

That *Other* DOD: Date of Diagnosis

It's not just the Date of Death that rocks your world when someone you love is terminally ill. Grief does not start with death—not when you get advanced warning that it's on its way. It starts the moment you learn there is no fixing the thing that's killing your spouse. The way you imagined the rest of your life, planned for it, dreamed of it . . . all of that changes in an instant.

As difficult as it is, talking about things when you know death is approaching really matters.

How you come to grips with this together as a

couple is what will prepare you both for what's coming. And in order to manage your grief, there's no hiding from it.

When Casper began to experience frequent choking from her worsening condition, she immediately told me there would be no feeding tubes, no hydration. Similarly, in the course of her career as a nurse, Linda had performed CPR on people with end-stage terminal diseases. She wanted none of that. They both wanted to see family. To say goodbye to our kids. To talk about their fears. To say thank you. And then, when it was time, to go as peacefully as possible.

You have to face what's happening—*together*—to make that possible.

I've seen families in hospice who don't want to talk about what's happening or even to tell their dying loved one that they are dying. It was not for me to say they had to do things differently, but in these cases, being unwilling to talk about what was happening left these people unable to say goodbye. What's more, the dying person did not get to decide for themselves what their end of life would be like. I saw time and again how this inevitably led to conflicts among family members about feeding tubes, CPR, medications, etc. All of this strife during an already painful time is so unnecessary.

Dying people know they are sick. They should be able to tell their loved ones what they want and don't want. They should be able to see that one special place, to call the people they love, and to say what is in their heart before it's too late. And when they can no longer speak for themselves but continue to hang on, you should have the peace of mind of knowing you are doing what they wanted.

In this chapter, I'll cover how to adapt to your new reality. First, we'll discuss acceptance. Then we'll move into how to manage your spouse's care, including how to get the best out of the healthcare system and how to talk to your doctor. A section with some specialized tips for same-sex couples has also been included, since I learned plenty about how the deck is sometimes stacked against us in the health-care system.

But before you we can get to any of that, first you need to wrap your head around what has just happened.

The Power of Acceptance

Your life has dramatically changed. One moment ago, your spouse was battling some weird symptom, or pain, or something was just wrong. Your goal was to find out what, and then to fix it.

But it turns out you can't. No one can. They are terminally ill. You are facing them dying.

Now what? How do you even begin to accept that your spouse, the person you promised "until death do us part," is going to use that part of the vows so soon? How do you adjust to this new reality while in the middle of a battle?

Here's the short answer. *You have no other choice.*

Neither do they.

This is going to be hard no matter what. But there are things the two of you can do to prepare for what lies ahead that will make it easier instead of harder.

Give yourselves a metaphorical minute to digest and process the information you've been given. And as big a shock as this is for you, remember it's an even bigger shock for your spouse, the person it's happening to directly. Be there for them in whatever way they need. And let them be there for you when they're ready. You're facing this *together*.

Once you both get over the initial shock of what's happening, now is the time to start talking to each other—honestly and openly. You have decisions to make. If you avoid these conversations now, then you —as your spouse's caregiver—may end up having to make these decisions alone, or risk being left out of them entirely. Maybe it's the social worker in me, but I find that doing this part together, and talking and using each of your best strengths is the way to get to really, truly accepting that this is what is happening.

If you don't, this disease and your spouse's death will take over your life, and it will happen in a way that leaves you with no time to say what needs to be said. No time to make things happen as you and your loved one would want them to be. This is never going to feel like a scene from some perfectly staged Lifetime movie-of-the-week, but if you really talk to each other right from the start, you can design the end to be whatever the two of you need it to be.

End of Life Discussion Points

So, what all do you need to talk about with your spouse? For starters, here are the bases to make sure you have covered.

- Do they want a second opinion about the diagnosis?
- Do they trust this particular doctor to take care of them and make the right decisions with them as they approach their death?
- What do they need to do to feel at peace before they die? A trip? A visit from someone? Letters to write, or phone calls to make?
- Is this catching up so quickly that your spouse will need to file for disability? (It's worth noting here that Social Security has a five-month wait to pay a claim if you are terminally ill, and that is *after* they process and approve the paperwork.)
- Does your spouse need to file for retirement in order to ensure posthumous benefits for the family?
- If there is going to be a retirement, do you need to plan some kind of recognition ceremony or celebration?
- If you don't already have a plan as a couple for your final arrangements (i.e., funeral, memorial, donor status, burial vs.

cremation, etc.), now is the time to make these decisions.

- If you'll be planning a service or memorial when the time comes, you'll need to decide on the location, as well as any music, readings, or people who will be asked to speak.

- You also need to make sure any legal paperwork that is needed is in order, and to do this as soon as possible. Is there going to be a Do-Not-Resuscitate (DNR) Order or Physician's Order for Life Sustaining Treatment (POLST)? Are you to be the decision maker listed on those documents in case your spouse is incapacitated? What does your spouse want if that becomes a reality?

- Who in your close circle—family and extended family—will need to be notified about what's happening and the decisions being made? In particular, how and when will you tell your kids, if you have them?

- You also need a plan to ensure your spouse will get the best and safest care while they are ill. Can you do it alone? Will your people help?

- And finally, does your spouse prefer to die at home with the help of in-home hospice care, or would they rather be in a hospice care facility?

There may be additional things you want to discuss or decide as a couple related to your cultural or religious traditions, family structure or history, or any number of other factors. But the above list applies to any couple in this situation as the "must discuss" topics.

You have to be at some point of acceptance to have these discussions. This acceptance will not be total until after your spouse has died. I have yet to meet a survivor who did not acknowledge that even if they were as ready as they could be, they did not fully understand it was really going to happen until they held their spouse's hand as they took their last breath. I also have not met anyone who could not remember that moment. No one says so in marriage advice books, but this is the most intimate moment that ever occurs in any marriage.

You won't want to miss it. And you won't want it clouded by anything left undone or unsaid.

Once you've had these important conversations and made your key decisions, the next part of adjusting to your spouse's terminal diagnosis is arming yourself with what you need to know to maximize their quality of life in the time they have left.

Knowledge Is Power

When you're facing a terminal diagnosis, it's all too easy to feel helpless. And you'll quickly find you're also facing a seemingly endless cavalcade of questions you need answers to as soon as possible. If you can't easily find those answers, it's time to get proactive. The more you know, the more both of you can make informed decisions. Only then will you know you're doing everything you can to stay on top of things.

Here's a list of best practice strategies you can use to manage your loved one's care by staying informed:

- Educate yourself. Read up on every credible source of information you can find about your loved one's illness and prognosis.
- What counts as a credible source? As a medical social worker and a caregiver spouse who has been through this process twice, I trust organizations that fit a specific criteria—namely that they have no vested interest in selling something or raising money. My go-to sources are the National Institutes of Health, associations for the illnesses being treated, the National Hospice and Palliative Care Organization, and social media groups run by families facing the same illness.
- Gather as much information as possible about your loved one's experience of the illness so that you are prepared to give your medical care team all of the information they need.
- What are your loved one's symptoms? Keep a journal of what these are when they occur.

- Be as accurate as possible with pain scales; some folks do not let on when they are in pain, or how much.
- Go back and think through recent history. Could there have been symptoms before you knew you were seeing them? If so, what were they, and when did they show up?
- Is there a family history of this illness or one that might be related? Have you asked?
- Communicate clearly and candidly with doctors and other medical providers.
- Be aware of any tendency in your loved one of not being entirely honest or forthcoming with doctors. If this is a concern, do your best to get word to the doctor about what is actually occurring.
- When dealing with dementia in particular, find a way to communicate with the treatment staff in a way that maintains the dignity of your loved one, and still allows you to fill them in on exactly what is occurring and what has changed.
- If desired, get a second opinion. Insurance companies normally allow access to this option, so use it if you don't feel you're being heard or if the diagnosis doesn't fit.
- Familiarize yourself with your health insurance. Get to know how your policy works so you can reach someone to appeal

to if you need equipment, treatment, a new doctor, or more tests. Everyone has a supervisor, and every state monitors their medical insurance companies.

- Get hooked into social media groups that are focused on whatever illness you are coping with, or suspect you are or will be dealing with. The advice from those already in the trenches is invaluable and is one of the best tools available to you to self-educate about the illness.

- Specifically, look for groups *not* funded by a pharmaceutical company. You want to find the boots on the ground folks who are dealing with this at home, not just in a sterile office environment.

- Be wary of groups that are anti-anything in particular. Case in point: if they hate meds, I am out. Meds help control symptoms. Same thing if they hate a particular kind of medical approach. I want to look at all the options.

- If they are a public forum, be cautious about what you say. Personally, I prefer private or secret groups where I can vent or find support without anyone else in the family seeing me, or having my posts show up publicly. I've found more help during a crisis at two in the morning from other families further along in the illness than from any association trying to tell me about their work for a cure no one will see for at least another twenty years.

Managing Care and Staying Organized

You want the best care for your spouse, but the health care industry can be incredibly difficult to navigate even under the best of circumstances. The same proactive approach you're taking to staying informed will help guide you here.

Even getting an appointment in a reasonable amount of time can be challenging, but with a terminal diagnosis, you don't have weeks or months to wait to see a specialist. Study up on what your policy actually says about your coverage, so you can make your providers toe the line. Otherwise, if you simply wait for each link in the chain to do their little bit, you may never get what you need in the time-frame you're working with. It's an unfortunate reality —and yet one you will need to radically accept—that being organized and on top of things in this situation includes managing those who are supposed to be managing your spouse's care. You have to get and stay organized.

In my experience, the best way to do this is to create a notebook that contains all of the information related to your loved one's diagnosis, symptoms, treatment, and care. This keeps all of that information in one place, so that you and any other caregivers who take over for you when you're not at home have all the information needed to ensure consistent quality of care.

You can organize this notebook in whatever way works best for you. I recommend one with titled dividers for different sections and a means of attaching outside information as needed, like doctor visit summaries and prescription details. Mark each section with a title so anyone can find the information they need quickly if you are not home.

The things that should go into this care management notebook include:

- Notes from all provider visits, in order by date and including the appointment time. What was discussed, and what symptoms were reported? What treatment did the doctor recommend or prescribe? Was a follow-up appointment scheduled? If so, when?
- A list of referrals, as well as when these visits are scheduled and completed.
- A section for copies of HIPAA release forms granting the primary caregiver (that's you) access to your loved one's medical information and records. You may need a separate form for each provider they see, so be sure to inquire about this. (Make sure a copy is filed with your insurance company too!)
- Notes about any calls you have made concerning your loved one's care, including

who you spoke to, dates and times, and any subjects discussed. This way if you are later told someone did not know something was needed, you can quote the time and date of previous discussions.

- A list of all your loved one's providers—pharmacy, doctors, hospitals, hospice, DME providers, other facilities, and any helpers. Include both addresses and phone numbers.
- Your address and phone number(s) should go on the front of the notebook. And if you go out of town on a business trip or for any other reason, be sure to include the name, phone number and address of where you're staying, as well as any other important information about travel arrangements, etc. Putting all of this front and center ensures that caregiver helpers can always get a hold of you quickly in a pinch.
- A medication information section that lists dosages; dates medications were started, adjusted or discontinued; pharmacy information; and what each medication was prescribed for.
- A list of the patient's allergies—this should also be placed toward the front of the notebook.
- A section related to doctor's orders and results.

- A section for labs and their results.
- A section for information related to appeals if your provider or insurance company refuses to grant something that is needed for the patient's care.
- A journal section for current symptoms. It's not necessary for this to be extensive, but it's practically impossible to track symptoms if you don't write them down. Take these notes with you to provider visits to be sure you can give a full account of current and past symptoms.
- A section for DNR/POLST documents. A Do-Not-Resuscitate (DNR) order is a simple document that indicates if a patient wants CPR or not. A Physician's Order for Life Sustaining Treatment (POLST) is a more comprehensive two-page document co-signed by your doctor. This document is normally printed on hot pink paper, which makes it easy to quickly identify. If included, both of these documents (DNR and POLST) should be placed somewhere they can be easily found in case 9-1-1 ever has to called while you're not at home. I recommend posting copies on the refrigerator with magnets, with additional copies in your cars, provider's records, at the hospital, and on you and your spouse at all times while out of the house.

Making calls to your doctor or insurance company when you need something can be frustrating, but having all the information you need on-hand will allow you to get straight to the point and stay on track. If they refuse to grant something you need, write down what was discussed and appeal the decision. It's much harder to deny services to a well-prepared spouse.

Use your insurance to your advantage. If you need something, call them. Ask if they have a case manager for very sick members. Use the Internet and help from friends, family, and neighbors to look for well-recommended specialists if you need them, and to find the best local hospice. Remember that every person in healthcare can be replaced, including your hospice. If you're not happy with their care, you have a right to change providers, ask for second opinions, and to appeal denials.

You are going to be tired and frustrated at times. You are also never going to forget that your loved one is dying, and this matters more to you than to any system. You may forget what needs doing or who you have called. That's where your notebook comes in. As their illness progresses, you will be your loved one's voice. Remember that when you hear a "no," what you should decide you're hearing instead is "We haven't realized who we're dealing with yet. But we will."

Give providers time limits and demand action. And remember that every person you speak to has a supervisor. I've gone so far as to stage a sit-in at my insurance gatekeeper's office. It worked!

How to Talk to the Doctor

In an ideal world, your doctor would be willing to say what needs saying without prompting. Unfortunately, that's not often the reality of the situation we're presented with as spouse caregivers. Doctors are not trained to have hard conversations, to talk about death, or to allow death to be the outcome of their treatment. They are trained to fight illness and provide hope. What you need right now is for your providers to be up front and brutally honest with you. This will be hard for them, and you will likely have to ask for this courtesy more than once.

You need to tell them what is going on at home, and they need to interpret it for you and tell you what it means. They're the one best equipped to recognize what stage you are now in and how much time you might have left with your spouse. If you feel like the doctor is not hearing what you're saying or what you think is going on, challenge them. *You* are the ones living with this illness, not your doctor. Ask them about the DNR, the POLST, and what other kinds of things you should be getting done right now. Make it clear that you know this is terminal and you need to be prepared.

All of that said, it is up to you to look for any signs your doctor is not being entirely honest, or isn't answering your questions directly. If they duck and cover when it comes to a DNR, you're in the wrong office. If they keep saying "there's always room for hope" or tell you that asking about time is morbid, walk away. You and your loved one need to know and need to be prepared. How do you plan a last trip if you really only have three weeks? I've seen friends go on last trips that were disasters because the communication with doctors was not clear enough.

Don't let this happen to you. Your family is facing an illness that is going to end in your loved one's death. You need to be prepared, to understand what will happen and when, and to have all of your affairs in order. You need to be confident in your doctor. Your loved one deserves that, and so do you. If your current provider is not providing this kind of peace of mind, there are others who will do better. That goes for hospices too. *You* are in charge. You can't stop what's coming, but you do get to decide how it will be managed and who helps you get to where you need to be.

Navigation Tips for Same-Sex Partners

I was hoping it would not be necessary to include this section. Until 2016, it looked like we were heading in the right direction and that the rights of same-sex couples would be respected more with each passing year. I no longer have confidence in that being the case.

In 1997, when Linda was first diagnosed with breast cancer, our first stop was surgery. She wanted a full mastectomy. We were in Florida, where we had zero legal rights as a couple. To counter this as best we could, we had powers of attorney, healthcare proxies, wills, and advanced directives. She put me down as her person on all her hospital forms. She told her surgeon in writing and verbally to tell me what the pathology results were.

That should have been sufficient, shouldn't it? Except for one thing. Did you catch the part about us being in Florida?

Linda came out of surgery and nobody told me.

I had a funny feeling, so I went and stood in the hallway outside the OR. I got there just before I saw her doctor heading down the hallway. Not only did he never call me in the waiting room—he *literally* ran around a corner to avoid me. So I went back to Linda's room, and the nurse receiving her on the med-surg floor wheeled her in, pushed the other bed in front of the door, and blocked me from entering.

I could hear Linda struggling, crying. I found another nurse who helped me push my way in, and we found the first nurse trying to convert Linda with prayer . . . with her arm over her head. In mastectomy land, that's dangerous. The nurse was a temporary float from the psych unit. We got her out of there, and Linda stabilized. Even after that, I had to wait twenty-four hours for the pathology report. Even with all of those documents we had gone to great lengths to have drawn up, we were treated with no regard for even basic medical care standards.

More recently, even here in much more gay-friendly California, Casper and I encountered similar problems at a hospital local to our area in 2012. At that point, she and I had most legal rights as domestic partners, though same-sex marriage was not legal at the time. We were checking her into a day surgery for a heart catheter. The registration clerk processed in another couple about our same age, then came to us. She immediately demanded our marriage license in order to treat us as a couple.

By that time, Casper had dementia and needed me there. Fortunately for that clerk, another staff person remembered me from Linda's treatment and warned her that I was the wrong person to mess with when it came to civil rights, and that I really would sue. She mentioned news channels and newspapers, and suddenly . . . we were a couple.

That should never happen. We should be past all of that. Unfortunately, we're not.

If you are a same-sex couple, be vigilant. Make sure you have your documents on file. Make sure HIPPA forms are signed to allow disclosure to you. Introduce yourselves as a couple. If you see another couple being treated differently than you, challenge it. There are always supervisors, house supervisors, and risk management folks you can contact. If there are relatives who will try to move you aside, be especially vigilant with those documents and instructions.

If you feel you are being treated without respect, you can change providers, but be sure to tell them why. Make it a learning experience, and maybe the next couple will have a better experience in a bad time.

The Best Worst Gift

Death is coming. I know it doesn't feel like it now, but advanced warning of this is a gift. You have some time to get your spouse's affairs in order, make them as comfortable as possible while they are ill, and arrange a peaceful ending to their life. To allow them to say goodbye. But you can't do these things if the two of can't face what's happening. Acceptance of this new reality is required to make the most of the time you have left together, to make this incredibly difficult thing that's happening *less difficult*. Stay informed, stay organized, and most of all, *talk* to each other. Support one another.

You're both grieving during this time, long before the day your spouse will take their last breath. So take care of yourselves. In the next chapter, we'll focus on how to help your spouse cope with their own grief about what's happening to them.

2

HELPING YOUR LOVED ONE COPE WITH THEIR OWN GRIEF

> Whatever you want to do, do it now. There are only so many tomorrows.
>
> — MICHAEL LANDON

Embrace A New Way of Looking at Life

Perspective changes everything. Receiving the news that your spouse is terminally ill is one of the single most devastating blows any of us can experience in our lives. And yet even so, this awful news comes with one of the most precious gifts imaginable.

Time. Time to do what must be done. Time to say what needs saying. Time to find some measure of acceptance. Time to say goodbye on our own terms.

It is never going to feel like *enough* time. That would mean having the power to press pause on what's happening and enjoy all the things you and your spouse have been looking forward to spending the rest of your lives doing together, for years and years to come. You may even be looking at less time than you were initially told at the time of the diagnosis. But you do have *some* time here, and it is yours and your spouse's to spend doing what you both need to make the most of it.

The only way to make this process work is to learn to adapt to what is happening day by day (and even hour by hour), and to do it as quickly as possible. Adapting is an art form you will perfect in the coming weeks or months. It is your new *modus operandi*.

If you can't adapt to what's happening, then you will not be able to take care of yourself or your spouse during what is likely to be one of the most painful and awful, but also potentially one of the most beautiful times in your life together as a couple. And yes, I said beautiful—because this time, while incredibly difficult, is also *so* special. Some of the most precious minutes, hours, and days of your marriage are right around the corner. That's what happens when love is tested and passes through fire. Your heart adapts because it has to.

Getting your head to follow your heart's lead can be more challenging. You must learn to adjust to the gauntlet of changes coming your way. You'll adapt to your spouse's deteriorating health and capacities, and to new responsibilities and your new role as a caregiver. You'll adapt to your own sense of grief and loss as it enters your life. And right now, it's time to help your spouse adapt to grieving their own looming death.

To do this, you'll have to be open about your own emotions while also giving them the space and support they need to process what's happening and how they feel about it. You need to make yourself ready to say the words, "I know you are going to die. I'm here for you. Let's do this together. I'm not going anywhere." And you have to mean them.

You see, that is what you meant when you promised "for better for worse, in sickness and in health." You may have thought you were just talking about the flu, but you were also talking about this.

You must be prepared to stand by and hold your loved one's hand. To let them say whatever they need to say. To let them cry or scream or rage, or even all three at the same time if that is what they require. You will adapt to their ever-shifting new reality in real time, just as they are doing. It may not be pretty, but if you allow it, it can include laughter, too.

In this chapter, we'll cover how to adopt the flexible mindset you'll need to cope with these difficult changes, how your spouse's waning energy level will affect their ability to cope and communicate, and how to help them process their experiences and feelings and to find closure where they need it. Finally, I'll share some tips born of my own experience for how to do all of this with as much grace under pressure as you can muster.

None of this is easy, but it's doable. Let's take it one step at a time.

Adjust Your Mindset to a New Life Expectancy

As you and your spouse move through the end of their illness and closer to their death, your ability to adapt together as a couple will be your saving grace. The words you use will be different. Plans for the future and the way in which you make them changes. There are no more long-term plans for trips or cele-brations. References to far-off graduations, wedding, or births can become uncomfortable. At our house, talk about the eventual arrival of grandchildren turned instead to talk of me telling our grandchildren about Linda— and later, both Linda and Casper—in the past tense.

A change in life expectancy changes absolutely everything about what you do, how you do it, how you talk about it, and who you want to spend your precious time with. Your new reality becomes a filter through which all of these things pass, altering and shaping how you will live your lives during this time.

One of the first things you will discover, as I did, is that not everyone around you is prepared to make this mental shift of radical acceptance and adaptation along with you. The simple reality you'll discover now is this: if certain people around you cannot accept and adapt to what's happening as you must, then they no longer fit in your life. Maybe later, but not right now. It's just too hard when you have your hands full taking care of your spouse, yourself, and any other close loved ones or dependents in the picture. Indeed, it can be surprising to learn who is and is not ready to go there with you when it comes down to it.

Likewise, it's okay to keep at arm's length any people in your life who hold very different religious or spiritual beliefs than you and your spouse if they feel the need to exert those beliefs now in a way that causes further pain or discomfort. Case in point? A very dear and well-meaning friend of ours kept telling Casper that she was lighting candles and that "God is going to find a miracle for you." Not only were we way past that point in our own process of accepting that Casper was dying of her illness, but Casper did not particularly believe in God. At the time, this friend's kindly meant comments were more hurtful than helpful.

Communication and Mood Changes

Another thing to prepare yourself for is adapting to fluctuations in your spouse's mood and energy level, and how that affects their capacity to engage with others. With many illnesses, the patient's daily energy level is further and further depleted, causing them to grow tired with any exertion as their disease overwhelms their systems. The resulting decreased capacity for socializing, or even talking much, can cause hurt for the people around them, especially those who are not around enough to see the gradual decline in progress and face a shocking change when they visit.

Pain meds add an extra layer of confusion at times, as does toxic build-up in the body as the liver or kidneys begin to fail. Medical problems that affect the brain's structures or its biochemistry can also cause sudden, seemingly inexplicable personality changes. This can be particularly upsetting and often happens with dementia patients in particular.

In our house, we became all too familiar with the ravages of dementia on the mind—both times around. One Monday during Casper's illness, I got a distressed call at work. "Come home," she said. "The animals are talking too loudly."

"Are they talking in cat and dog, or people?" I asked her.

"People," she said. "But I can't make out what they are saying. I'm trying to understand but I can't." She couldn't tell if they were talking out loud or just in her head either.

Other days she raged, not wanting to be touched or spoken to, or having lost track of time and convinced that I was staying away on purpose long after when I said I'd be home. She feared taking care of her was too much for me and that I would inevitably abandon her before the end—no matter how lovingly I reassured her otherwise.

When the mind and body are thrown into chaos in the late stages of a terminal illness, moods and one's grasp on reality can shift all over the place, often revolving around the dying person's internal struggle with fear, anger, sadness, loss, anxiety, or other difficult emotions. Even when Casper was upset or angry about something that *hadn't actually happened*, the emotions themselves were real and had to be dealt with. Your spouse will more often than not still need you to comfort and steady them during these times, to make them feel safe without judgment.

Depending on the type of illness your spouse has, memory loss may be another reality for you to bend and adapt to during this time. Nobody wants to lose their memory. It's scary, and the person it is happening to can tell from the expression on your face that they are causing you distress, even if they don't currently know who you are. One of the members of the dementia support group I joined coined a term my team and I all use now, which we teach to new families facing dementia: fiblet.

A fiblet is what you tell when you have to lie to not cause distress, to keep from challenging your spouse's current reality. Memory loss can combine with mood shifts and turn into wildly out-of-character suspicion and accusations. I must warn you that I rarely meet a fellow widow who was not accused of poisoning and stealing from their late spouse if dementia or other memory problems were in play. Thinking that you are cheating on them is also common. Both Linda and Casper accused me of poisoning them at the end, and Casper was sure I was cheating on her with one of my best friends. She was horrified when she realized what she'd said later.

Changes in behavior, mood, communication, and

personality can be hard enough to deal with just for you and anyone else who lives with you and your spouse, but you'll also have to prepare those friends and family who come to visit. I recommend sending a periodic email to all of those who might visit with a brief update including a description of current out-of-character behaviors and how to respond to them. An informed visitor makes for a better visit—for everyone.

And at some point, these visits become even more important, since they become the means by which your spouse is able to say goodbye to the people they care for.

Complete Relationships, Especially the Challenging Ones

One of the most important factors in your spouse being able to adapt to and process their own grief is making sure they have opportunity to complete the important relationships in their life before they pass on. This is just as important for the people they are close to.

In a nutshell, completing relationships happens in one of two ways. You either do it before someone dies, or the griever left behind manages it alone. It's not hard to guess which option is easier and more beneficial for both of you. In my line of work, I spend most of my time with grief clients working on finishing relationships after their loved one has died. Having to do it this way makes things so much harder. What's more, it can cause additional and wholly unnecessary emotional pain for the person who is dying.

Your spouse has a long list of people they have touched in their lifetime. As the two of you prepare for the end, one of the best ways to encourage them to talk about their death and what concerns them is to ask who they need to see so they can say goodbye. It then becomes your job to try to get those people to come. You also may need to shield your spouse from knowing that there are people who will *not* come, for whatever reason. Here, telling fiblets may become a necessity.

We all have things we need to say, hear, and apologize for, and to offer gratitude for what that relationship has meant to us. This applies to every important relationship in your spouse's life—including the one you share together. If things are left hanging, it makes the grief process infinitely more difficult. Knowing that you didn't apologize for something, or tell them one more time just how much their love meant to you, or what parts of them would always be part of you. That unfinished business will follow you, wake you up at night, and can drag you down. If you have time to say it, don't waste the opportunity.

For those who will not come, or cannot get there, you have some options. FaceTime, online chats, even online discussion forums can offer another way to say goodbye and complete relationships. If someone is willing to participate, you can make it happen. If the technology is not available, even just reading a letter from that person to your spouse and recording their response is an option.

Now, you may have very strong feelings about the people your spouse needs to see who will not come through your door. Your spouse doesn't need to know this, and you don't need to hold onto it—in the long run, those feelings will not serve either of you. If they are slipping in and out of awareness, you can tell your spouse that someone who refused to come was there, that they visited and said goodbye, or that you were not able to wake your spouse but the visit happened, and the person sent their love and said what they needed to. If this can ease your spouse's heart or mind and make their final transition easier, it's worth doing. You have can have your spouse write or dictate a letter or record a short video if they need to say something to that person.

What you don't want is your spouse trying to hang on for a goodbye that will never come, or to die feeling that they did not get to say something that really mattered to them. Saying goodbye is a powerful moment. Do your best to make these moments happen.

Manage Difficult Changes as Gracefully as You Can

So, how do you manage all these adaptations and changes as capacities shift in your home? For me it was one step at a time. I tried to be as graceful as I could as I moved things around, added visitors who were friends to our crew of caregivers and sitters, and took away the keys. When we had to have friends come to sit with Casper, I made it festive, or they would volunteer to bring in a meal that they used to enjoy together. I rearranged our bedroom to make room for visitors, so they could sit and watch TV with Casper in the hospital bed. We joked as we emptied catheter bags. Given the choice, laughter was better than anger or tears.

When reduced capacities meant that Linda could not tolerate long visits that we knew would be emotional, I set limits on how long these would be. Linda asked me to do this, but did not want her family to know how tired she was, so I sent out emails with visiting instructions. It hurt some feelings, but it allowed her to rest and still see the people she wanted to spend time with. I arranged furniture on our front lawn so she would not have to walk more than a few steps when she went outside to visit. Likewise, I added furniture to the living room so more people could join her there.

I told anyone who wanted to see her that they needed to come to us so Linda would not be completely worn out by the time we made an hour trip across town. And I made sure that she was never so worn out from others that she didn't have energy for our kids. When you are facing the end of the time you will have, the immediate family—however you define this—deserves the best time.

Aside from giving them the space and support they need to talk about what they're feeling, one of the most important things you can do to help your spouse grieve is to make sure they know you're going to be okay after they're gone. It will be hard, but you'll get through it. Don't say things like you cannot live without them, cannot go on without them, or that they can't die. They are going to die. The question is whether you will give them what they need to prepare and to let go easily when the time comes.

They need to know your life doesn't end when theirs does. Your spouse needs to see you adapting and preparing so they do not have the biggest worry of every dying spouse—that their death is going to harm you or kill you, too. If they can see how they will live on in you and be remembered, and that you will indeed be okay, they can begin to grieve the way they need to in order to get through this. Only then can they prepare to let go and find peace with what's happening to them.

And that is a gift beyond measure.

3
___

YOUR NEW ROLE AS A CAREGIVER

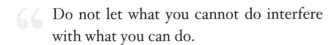 Do not let what you cannot do interfere
with what you can do.

— JOHN WOODEN

Self-Care for Caregivers

Once you become a caregiver for your spouse,
you will hear a lot of folks tell you to "take
care of yourself." Even when we're not mid-crisis and
life is just busy and hectic, we know we *should* take
good care of our physical, mental, emotional, and
spiritual health. Still, many of us fall short on these
fronts. And when you're in the midst of learning how
to take care of a dying spouse, it can seem especially
impossible to take time for yourself.

Here's the kicker. *You have to*. If you don't, it could
literally kill you. It's well-established that caregivers

who fail to look after their own needs while caring for a dying spouse have a much stronger likelihood of, at worst, not surviving the loss of their loved one, or at least risking permanent damage to their health and wellbeing.

If not addressed, physical strain experienced before your loved one's death can drastically impact not only the severity of your grief, but also your physical health. Researchers Schulz and Beach observed that, "after adjusting for age, sex, race, education, and stressful life events, strained caregivers of a disabled spouse were at a 63 percent higher risk for all-cause mortality over a four-year period than those without a disabled spouse."[1] They went on to note that highly strained caregivers were nearly twice as likely to die within roughly this same time frame than less strained caregivers, and that this heightened risk effect was seen to occur across race and sex demographic groups.

In other words, this experience hits everyone hard, no matter who you are. And it you don't take care of yourself now, you may be cutting your own life short. Your loved one needs to be able to count on you to be there for them during this time, and you owe it to them and to yourself to make sure you're going to be okay in the long run once they're gone. This is only possible if you practice good self-care throughout this process.

But what does that even mean? How do we take care of ourselves during this incredibly difficult time? What does it look like? How do you do it?

It means a lot of different things, but most of all it means learning to be more aware of not just your spouse's needs during this time, but your *own*. What do *you* need to get through this? More, once you've attained awareness of what you need, you have to ask for it. Sometimes you'll also need to *fight* for it.

In this chapter, we'll cover how to achieve a greater awareness of your needs and how to go about getting those needs met so that you don't do lasting harm to yourself during this time. This includes setting healthy boundaries, how to talk to friends and family, and giving yourself the space you need to grieve this loss while it's happening. I'll also go over how to set realistic expectations for yourself and when it's most important to lean into your support network.

First up, let's define what self-care as a caregiver looks like.

Identify Your Needs

The first step in taking care of yourself right now is to start figuring out what you need to maintain your physical, mental, emotional, and spiritual health during this time. So, let's briefly break down each one of these categories.

Physically, it's your job to keep your body healthy. You'll be tapping into your deepest reserves of energy while caring for your spouse, so getting enough rest to function, eating healthy, staying hydrated, and getting at least a little exercise in where you can is more important than ever right now. And just because you're shuttling your loved one back and forth to the doctor doesn't mean you get to skip going yourself. Stay on top of your preventative care and any health issues of your own.

To practice good mental health self-care, avoid isolating yourselves while your spouse is ill. You each need someone—or better yet, a circle of people—to talk to about what you're going through, someone who will really listen and be supportive. Be aware though, that some people are just not capable of hearing intimate medical details or coping with difficult emotions. Caregiver support groups—either in person or online—are a great resource. If you have a history of depression or anxiety, a therapist might be a good idea, too. Be sure to find one with experience in end of life and grief.

Good emotional self-care means being aware of and giving yourself space to feel and express your emotions in a constructive rather than destructive way. It also means showing kindness and patience to yourself—which for many of us, is *much* harder than showing kindness and patience to others. Setting realistic expectations for yourself and others, as well as setting healthy boundaries around your needs are also crucial components in conserving your emotional energy. We'll cover this in more detail later in this chapter.

Your spiritual health can be attended to by participating in religious services or your religious community, having a creative outlet, or even just giving yourself the time and space to take a walk in nature every now and then. Find whatever it is that feeds your spirit and helps you replenish the well from which you draw your physical, mental, and emotional energy, and make time for this where you can.

Check in with yourself regularly to assess how you feel on all four of these fronts. Have any new needs come up? If so, honor them. Most importantly, raise your white flag when you need help. Spell out exactly what you need. But how do you start these sometimes difficult conversations?

How to Talk to Friends and Family About What's Happening

Talking to friends and family to make them aware of what is happening in your world right now can be challenging. That's a nice way of saying *some people may not want to know*. Indeed, you may become frustrated with their responses if you find they are not hearing you or not honoring what you and your spouse need. The thing is, when you are busy with a spouse who is losing ground and is going to die, you get to set the rules.

This is the biggest loss you will experience as a couple. One day soon, you will not have your spouse here with you anymore. The rest of the people in your lives need to hear both of you. This means it is up to you to communicate what is happening and what you need.

Actually *doing* the communicating, though, can be

so tough as to feel all but unapproachable at first. Nobody wants to hear you say that death is approaching and it's time to get ready. Nonetheless, trust me when I say nobody will forget if you do not allow them the time they need to prepare. You are caught in a bind on this one.

So, here is my best from the ground, boots-on advice: give yourself permission to muck it up a bit. Forgive yourself in advance for that moment when you find yourself telling someone in a way they do not like or simply do not want to hear. There are going to be hurt feelings. Your spouse, their friend or loved one, is dying. They do not want this to be happening any more than you do.

Your job, should you accept it, is to do the telling. Let them cope by finding solace through their other support systems—*not* by crying on your shoulder. Yours is the primary loss here, and you do not have the time or emotional energy to figure out each person's individual needs or desires. That's not realistic during this time, and it's not fair for anyone to expect otherwise.

Use whatever communication methods work best for you. If the next person you need to tell is someone you know will exhaust you on the phone or in person, send a text or an email, or have someone else tell them for you. Have a large network of extended family or friends? Use a group email.

Once you've broken the news to people, you can update them with new information as things change by blog, email, or phone chain. Facebook groups are also helpful in keeping people in the loop and can be created to be private. The bottom line here? Find whatever way of communicating is easiest for you and do it that way.

People will offer to help, but typically in a nebulous way that doesn't make it any easier to actually *ask* them for help when you need it. I finally developed a list of thoughtful gestures I could use help with and just forwarded that to people who offered to help. My list included:

- Come over to do a few loads of laundry, including folding it
- Tackle my yard work
- Run errands for me
- Cook and deliver meals (in disposable dishes that can be frozen)
- Take my kids out for a fun day (with instructions to *not* talk to the kids about their dying loved one unless they bring it up first)
- Just sit and listen to me over a cup of coffee, and let me feel heard

Your list might look different, but I highly encourage you to make one to just be able to send to people. Being specific about the help you need will get you better results.

When talking to friends and family about what's going on and what you need right now, it's okay to also spell out what you *don't* need and *don't* want, which brings us to our next topic: how to set healthy boundaries.

Set Healthy Boundaries

While talking to friends and family about what's going on, it's vital to set expectations and limits about what works and doesn't work for your family right now.

Perhaps the most important way to do this during this time is to create rules about visiting. Make it clear that visitors should not to expect someone who is in the end stages of life to go out and do the visiting. It exhausts them to leave the house, and it wears out the caregiver. Your loved one needs to use their remaining strength for the activities *they* choose, and that means visitors need to come to them. As a note, being made to understand that things have progressed this far is often one of the ways in which people in your extended circle will finally start to process that your spouse is truly dying.

At home, you are responsible for ensuring that visitors will not cause unnecessary fatigue, stress, or pain for your spouse. Well-meaning friends and family may say things out of ignorance or emotional discomfort that can cause unintended harm. It's perfectly acceptable to talk to visitors ahead of time about what is and is not okay to discuss during their visit. A list of prohibited topics should include:

- Placing blame for your spouse's illness or impending death
- Sharing horror stories of people who had or died of similar illnesses
- Suggesting that God will "work a miracle" and cure your dying spouse
- Recommending miracle cures (i.e., vitamins, health foods, alternative or experimental therapies) or otherwise suggesting that you and your spouse haven't already exhausted every possible avenue of treatment
- Comparing their own losses to this upcoming one
- Asking about inheritances or ashes

Those who fail to respect your family's boundaries should not be allowed to make another visit until they agree to abide by your rules. Similarly, your spouse should not feel obligated to spend their precious remaining time and energy on visits with people they either don't care to be around or who in any way make them feel worse. When folks visit too long, tell them that you have to preserve energy for others and that it is time to go. It may feel harsh, but it's honest and necessary.

Then there are boundaries that also extend to you, and to your kids if you have any at home.

None of you should be expected to expend your energy helping to make others outside of your family feel better about things right now. This is a time when others should be supporting and taking care of *you and your family* while you support and take care of your spouse—not the other way around.

For this reason, if there are people in your life who make demands on your time and energy (or your kids') or expect you to make this okay *for them* right now, it's time to put a boundary in place that this is not okay—not right now. Set your limits. Tell these folks what you need from them, even if it's just to give you some space while you're getting through this. And again, if there are people who can't respect your boundaries right now, a little healthy distancing goes a long way.

Setting and sticking to boundaries with other people is crucial to taking good care of yourself and your loved one right now. But it's just as important to set healthy expectations for yourself about your impending loss.

Give Yourself Permission to Grieve Now

When you're a caregiver for someone with a terminal illness, grieving happens long before your loved one dies. We call this *anticipatory grief*—and it is exactly what it sounds like. You are anticipating their death and grieving it beforehand.

It's only natural that while watching someone you love lose ground to their illness over time, you will start to grieve with every little loss. Your spouse will too. If you can talk about it together, you can create a space for healing old hurts, and for saying what you need to say to each other before they die. Leaning into this process with honest and compassionate communication can create a new kind of intimacy for both of you.

Anticipatory grief for the spouse being left behind means beginning to come to terms with this approaching death in the time you still have left *before* it actually happens. It also means letting yourself start to think ahead to what comes next. Those who begin to prepare for this transition early on will do better and be healthier after their loved one dies. A prepared widow is one who can plan the reorganization of her new life to come, and who takes time to consider what she wants that life to look like.

You know what I most wish someone had told me as a grieving widow-to-be? I wish I had known to give myself permission to not feel guilty about what is a necessary process in facing the terminal illness of my spouse. Yes, there were times that I thought about what my life would be like after Linda died. I needed to convince myself that I would be able to get up in the morning, get the kids ready, and make sure the pets wouldn't starve. While I was still grappling with the immense challenges of the *before*, I needed to know there would be an after.

Linda and I had conversations about trips I might take, getting to see friends without the worry of being exhausted from lugging around oxygen tanks. We occasionally even talked about the possibility that she might be right in her insistence that I should eventually remarry. After all, I was going to be forty-six years old when I became I widow. Half of my life was still ahead of me.

We talked about a future for me that held far less stress—no more medical equipment, doctors, or waiting. The kids would no longer have to worry about Mama dying while they were at school, afraid that they wouldn't be there. I began to see a time ahead when I could focus on my studies, take my exams, and finally get my professional license, because I was going to need more income to support our family as a single-income household.

When all was said and done, the plans I made during this time, along with the grieving that Linda and I did together while she was still with me, carried me through some of my most painful moments after she died. It also helped me prepare to reorganize and reclaim my life—for being able to even see myself as still *having* a life. It was Linda who made me promise to get my license done, and Linda who told me to marry Casper.

Thinking about what I needed in order to get through what was coming wasn't easy. It wasn't something I particularly wanted to do. But it's what set me on the path to actually being a successful and happy person who is also a widow, someone with a life yet to live on the other side. Even so, I couldn't have gotten there alone. I needed the support of the other important people in my life to help me find a path through this difficult time.

Lean In

'Support system' is a favorite term among social workers. We assess them in our work. We set them up for ourselves and our family members on instinct. And when we are facing a terminal illness at home, we lean on this circle of trusted friends and family, lean into them and count on them. We may not do this often, but when do, we *really* do.

My main support during this time was my lifelong friends. I'm lucky to have an incredible group of girlfriends who have been in my life since elementary school. In addition to them, I have a group best friends who refer to ourselves collectively as our "tribe," three couples with seven kids between us. When trouble brews, a tribal council is called. As an example, a few years ago we all had to cancel a planned cruise because one member had a stroke the week before we were scheduled to leave. Instead of going on vacation without that family, the entire tribe spent that week in ICU together, and our kids supported one another. These are the groups I drew from in creating my support system to get through first Linda's death, and later Casper's.

If you don't know already, figure out who these people are in your life and let them know you're going to need their help. The sooner, the better. Assign roles and know who you can count on to not to be afraid of the dying process, or of grief. Once you do, your new reality becomes so much easier.

So how did I, as a notoriously do-it-all-myself

type ask for help? Well, it wasn't easy, but I did it because I realized I had no choice. I simply couldn't do it all on my own. In particular, I needed people I trusted to come stay with Linda—and later, Casper—while I was working or traveling for work so they would be safe.

The day that hospice called and said they were on the way to the house to care for Linda, my work friends, including my boss, simply packed my stuff up and sent me home. When she was in her last week, they showed up with matzo ball soup, fresh flowers, and help. My church friends came to spend time with the kids. In other words, when there was a need, I had someone who could step up if I only asked.

I *learned* to ask. I had to.

You will too. And the more you make a practice of asking for help when and where you need it, from the people you know you can count on, the easier it gets.

Now that you have a handle on what you'll need to be an effective caregiver—of your own needs as well as your spouse's—the next thing we need to tackle is how to make the most of the time the two of you have left as a couple.

4

MAXIMIZE THE TIME YOU HAVE LEFT TOGETHER

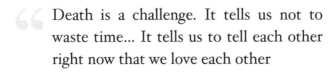

> Death is a challenge. It tells us not to waste time... It tells us to tell each other right now that we love each other
>
> — LEO BUSCAGLIA

Time to Make New Memories

When the person you love is dying, it's so important to celebrate the good times you've had together and make new memories while you still can. There's a lot about this process that is just plain awful. That means it's even more important to be able to make and hold onto good memories of this time too. Just like you've gotten through every other struggle that has come your way as a couple, you're going to get through this too.

In the time you have left together, you get to

choose how to spend your time to make the very most of it. It's your last time to talk, hold hands, and walk through favorite memories. You'll want to make it count. Ironically, this can create pressure on both of you to try to do too much, include too many people at the expense of your own intimate moments, and make this time "perfect."

Let's think about that. Have you ever made any one thing absolutely perfect? Is it realistic to try to do that now, with everything else on your plate? Do you want your memories of this time to be colored by stress and disappointment in yourself for not doing it right—whatever that means?

The answer to all of those questions, if we're being really honest with ourselves, is a resounding nope. And that means that now is the time to keep your expectations about this time period realistic. Both of you need to focus on what you *can* do, within reason and while being compassionate to yourselves and your needs. The way to do that is to allow yourself to be truly present in the moment with what's happening *right now*, week to week and day by day. This means making sure that the best of this time— not to mention the lion's share of your spouse's dwindling energy—is spent on making good memories with each other first, and *then* with the rest of the people who truly mean the most to you.

In this chapter we're going to cover strategies to help you make the most of this time: empowering yourself to do what you need to, but not more than that. That means deciding how you want to spend your time and how much you will need to limit the things and relationships that are going to get in the way of that right now. We'll look at how to empower your loved one to have a say in how they will spend their remaining time and how they can play an active role in what happens at the end of their life. Finally, we'll talk about how to keep your sense of humor— yes, even now, *especially* now—and why you're going to need it.

Empower Yourself

'Empower yourself' is a weird phrase. At face value, it sounds like you're meant to be adding batteries or something. It can also sound like therapist-speak. In a sense, it is. But it's also a much-needed mindset at this time in your life. You need to claim and use your power in order to manage your life and your partner's illness and death. If you don't, others will. There are important decisions to be made, and they need to come from the two of you.

There's so much pressure from others during this stressful time to do or say things a certain way. We've talked about the importance of deciding what you need—both individually and together—to face what's coming and say goodbye in a way that's uniquely right for the two of you. Now is the time to actually make that happen.

Are there any remaining things that your spouse can still do that would mean something special for you, both now and after? Do you need to simply shut the door for a bit and make a video on your phone of the two of you saying you love each other?

It's important for your wellbeing to be able to step back and remove yourself from the rest of the world and do what you need to for and with each other. You may offend a few people. That's okay. They're not the one losing their spouse.

Empowering yourself now will mean feeling better able to be in charge of your own grief process —both now and later. And it will mean you get to finish what you need to do. Some of what you need to do to make the most of this time together might not even directly involve your spouse. It may mean some time with your best friends, your kids, or your pets. Or it may mean you simply need some time alone to be inside your own head without interruption. At the end of the day, being there for yourself means you can be there for and with your partner.

Whatever time you need, and however that need manifests, *take it*. Give yourself that chance to take ownership, take a breath, and recharge your batteries. Once you can feel prepared to make your own decisions, for your own good, you will be able to prepare those around you for the next phase. And you will have the time you need right now—precious time while your spouse is still here that you will never get back once it's spent.

Empower Your Loved One

Equally important to empowering yourself is empowering your spouse. This is not the time for them to focus their limited time and energy fulfilling perceived obligations to others. On the contrary, they should be spending what time and energy they have left doing whatever they need to leave this life feeling at peace. Maybe that means spending time with close friends and loved ones, completing a few more "bucket list" dreams or goals, or pursuing a cherished hobby as long as they are still able to do it.

However they choose to spend it, the important thing is that the time they have left should feel *lived*.

One thing that helped Linda make the most of her time left was writing her own obituary and creating a memorial video. To some, such things may sound morbid. But you have to look at it from the perspective of someone looking at the last remaining months and weeks of their lifetime, once they have accepted what's coming. When this is your reality, knowing that you gave shape and form to the things your loved ones will remember you by can be incredibly empowering. My long-time friend Wendy took on the task of helping Linda with both of these projects—one of the most precious gifts she ever could have given to Linda and to me.

Just as your spouse needs a strong say in how they live the remaining days of their lives, they also need to be empowered to have a say in how their death will occur. This allows for a peaceful transition, since they can rest easy knowing *you* know what their wishes are and that you will fulfill them. For example, Linda wanted to spend her final days downstairs in our living room, so she could see and interact with anyone who came in. On the opposite end of the spectrum, Casper craved privacy and solitude, so she stayed upstairs in our room.

Linda was aware to the very end, and she needed to have control over as much as she could. She decided when she would use the hospital bed and where it would be. She chose her environment, her music, the videos we would watch as she made her final memories with the kids.

If your experience ends up anything like mine—twice over—you will have plenty of people chiming in thinking they know what's best when it comes to these kinds of decisions. But at the end of the day, the only person's opinion who matters is your spouse's. It's their death, and that means it's their choice. What's more, they need to know they can trust you to stand up for them and carry out their wishes once they are past the point of being able to physically speak up for themselves.

This trust in your steadfastness to your spouse's wishes is what will allow you to create the space they need to finally let go when the time comes.

Keep Your Sense of Humor

You might think I'm crazy on this one, but hear me out here. Yes, you are entering what will be one of the most difficult, stressful, and heartbreaking periods of your lifetime. And that's exactly why, as much as humanly possible, it's vital right now to keep your sense of humor intact. There is a reason that the funniest people on the planet are those who often come from places of great personal pain. That's because humor is humanity's first and last, *best* way of defusing and finding a way to cope with the things that hurt us.

The ability to find and see the lighter side of our tribulations in life is one of the greatest blessings any of us can bestow on ourselves. And this is no less true for you right now. If anything, *it's more true now than ever*.

To get through what's coming, you and your spouse will need your senses of humor. You may also find that the two of you increasingly find greater pleasure in gallows humor than you did before, and if that's the case, more power to you. Don't let anyone tell you that's not appropriate or not okay. Whatever gets the two of you through this in a way that's helpful is a *good thing*.

As someone who has worked in hospice, I can tell you that folks who are called to serve in this way have the most profoundly disturbed sense of humor you will find in anyone, *ever*. If you don't experience death on a daily basis, you certainly may not see the humor that can come during such times, or understand that recognizing these moments of humor in no way lessens each person's passing as a sacred moment. For us, humor walks hand in hand with that sense of the sacred, *lifting* it. We have to allow this in order to survive the daily life we live.

So, take a page from our playbook and let humor serve you and your spouse in this way now.

Experiencing the decline and death of someone you love dearly puts a great strain on you. There is no way around it. And if you're not careful, that strain can make you sick. Did you know that science has shown that humor changes our brain chemistry by reducing stress hormones? If you let it, laughter will be your saving grace. You are not laughing *at* your loved one. You are laughing *with* them, or at the situation. Set the tone, and don't allow anyone to tell you that you are being disrespectful. You are taking care of yourself, and the reduction in your stress level will help not just you, but will actually help reduce your spouse's stress too. It's a win-win.

How to Support Your Kids Through This

I have a therapist friend who recently lost her husband. At the time, she had little kids at home and one on the way, and the first thing she asked was, "How do I do this?"

In my line of work, I've learned the importance of educating children before a death occurs so they understand the physical process. Once they understand what is going to happen, they don't have to be afraid of it. Kids need to be talked through whatever feelings they are having, rather than keeping it pent up inside or being allowed to think something they feel is wrong. And you can't tell them "it's going to be okay" because, in that moment, *it's not.*

Some folks may balk at discussing the harsh reality of death with a child. But if you don't, you run the risk of having to focus entirely on a distressed child rather than your spouse, and on how others react to your child reacting, and having to *save* your child from well-meaning people who want to swoop in but who are not exactly on your child's list of favorite people.

Plan ahead. Be ready. Help your kids be ready. They can't stop what's coming any more than you can.

When we were losing Linda, I assigned each of our children an adult of their own—someone each of them loved and trusted—to keep an eye out for distress, upset, anger, really *anything* that looked out of place for that kid and their personality. Each person I put in this role knew their assigned kiddo well enough to spot pending trouble. Knowing that each of our children had someone focused just on them during this time allowed me to focus on Linda in the way both of us needed.

Kids need to say goodbye too, and in their own way. They don't need an audience or any coaching. They just need time and space, so if there is time, give that to them. Give them private time with your spouse. If they are willing, ask them to write down what their parent told them during these times. Chances are they won't remember later if they don't write it down, and these final conversations are so special and important. Even so, if they say they don't want to, don't push. You can also ask your spouse to record a video or to write such things down for the kids to have forever, or even have them dictate such things to you or someone else they trust.

Do your best to give your kid their real life back in the midst of everything. If they have a game, send them to it. If it's prom season, send them shopping for a dress. You can ask for help from your tribe in getting these things accomplished. But your children are, after all, still children. They need life to be normal where it still can be. My mom discovered purple hair dye and shops popular with teenagers when Linda was dying. She got time with her grand-kids, and they got to get out of the house. Their friends still came over and got to say goodbye too. Then they all hopped in the pool.

Have a plan for where the kids will be when your spouse's death occurs. Should your kids stay and watch their parent's body being removed by the mortuary, or not? In our house we decided this was simply too much for our kids. So our plan was to send them out for ice cream, because ice cream fixes everything, and because it's one thing to sit on a bed and be part of your parent's death, and another to see your parent becoming a body to be taken away.

More than anything, give your child a voice, and listen when they use it. They are wiser than we give them credit for being.

Memories are Forever

Toward the end while Casper was dying, there was one night when her mind was clearer than it had been in some time. That night, our kids piled onto the bed with her, Kerry perched as close to Casper as she could get. The rest of the room was filled with the people in our lives who Casper loved and who loved her—good friends, favorite coworkers, family. Everyone who wanted to got the chance to say something they valued about Casper.

Casper heard the love in what each person said, took it in, and was able to give that love back. She was glad we'd had the time to be a family, and she got to express that to each person in the room.

The opportunity for moments like this is something I wish for all families going through this kind of impending loss. The person who is dying needs to hear about the positive impact they've had on the lives of the people who mean the most to them. And as for the rest of us? We need a chance to make sure that person knows just what they mean to us when we can still look them in the eye and tell them so.

Having that time, that experience with someone you love before they leave this world is incalculably precious. Not only does it give them a sense of closure as they near the end, but it will be a boon to your grieving heart once they are gone. Yes, this time is impossibly hard. But you might be amazed at how it can bring you closer with unexpected, stolen moments of joy, laughter, and warmth.

Get as much mileage out of those moments as you can. They will warm your heart and spirit for years to come.

In order to fully enjoy this time, it's important to familiarize yourself with what will happen from here on out. In the next chapter, you'll learn about hospice care and the services they provide. Hospice is going to become an invaluable resource to you and your family. The sooner you understand how, the more prepared you'll be to take full advantage of what they have to offer and the more you'll be able to set your mind at ease that your spouse will be properly taken care of in their final days.

5

HOSPICE CARE 101

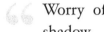 Worry often gives a small thing a big shadow.

— AUTHOR UNKNOWN

The Beginning of the End

The news that hospice is on its way to your home can be startling. It means the time your loved one has remaining is now drawing to a close. But the arrival of hospice can also give you a sense of relief. And I'm here to tell you that if you feel some relief here, that is 100 percent okay.

Your spouse's suffering is nearing an end. The uproar that has replaced the life you had before is winding down to a stop. You've spent so much time and energy trying to find proper care, fighting for the services your loved one needs, standing in line at pharmacies, and filing countless sets of paperwork. And then there is the emotional labor you've been tasked with on top of all of that: making decisions, setting healthy limits, coming to terms with all of the changes you have made and are still going to have to make.

When you take all of this into consideration, it's no surprise why caregivers experience some relief at this point in the process. Through all of this, you've been carrying an impossibly heavy load. Now is the time to let a trusted team of trained professionals take some of that weight from your shoulders.

The idea of hospice often seems scary to those who are unfamiliar with how it works. The most common misconception is that the goal is to speed up the patient's death. The truth is that your hospice team is there to ensure that your spouse is as comfortable as anyone can possibly make them, and that they are able to die with dignity in their own time and in their own home, supported and cared for around the clock. Having professionals there to manage your spouse's final care means you can refocus your energy and just be a spouse right now instead of having to be both a spouse and the primary caregiver.

When it's done right, hospice is the most effective medical program in the country. It incorporates all of the care the patient needs, all at home. The doctor, nurses, home health aides, chaplains, social workers, and volunteers all come to you. Even the pharmacy and DME companies deliver on demand.

Need morphine at two in the morning? It's there.
More oxygen? On the way.

Hospice also exists to educate you, your spouse,
and any visitors who come into the home about what
is happening and what to expect, as well as best prac-
tices based on their wealth of experience being of
service to people who are dying and their families. If
you let them, your hospice team will provide
emotional, spiritual, and medical support from the
moment they arrive until after your loved one dies.

In this chapter, I'll walk you through the ins and
outs of what services are provided by hospice, who all
is involved in this process, and what to expect when
they show up at your door. Understanding more
about how hospice works will mean less worry for
you during a very stressful time. And it will also allow
you to make the most of the services being provided
to you, your spouse, and the rest of your loved ones.

First up, since there are a lot of misconceptions
floating around about it, let's talk about what hospice
is and what it isn't.

What Exactly is Hospice?

In a nutshell, hospice is a medical program that
provides essential end-of-life services. It supports not
just the person who is dying, but their immediate
family and caregiver(s) too.

Hospices can come to your home and provide
services there, or they can provide services in another
facility that provides a specific subset of services, like

long-term care, board and care, memory care, or a skilled nursing facility. In any of these types of facilities, hospice acts as a supplement to the care already present. They also continue to provide emotional support and bereavement support for you after your spouse dies.

It's important to understand that hospice is a *guaranteed* Medicare benefit, and that Medicaid and MediCal provide this benefit as well. Most insurance companies mirror the same benefit, and full-scope programs under the Affordable Care Act (ACA) also cover hospice. If you have private insurance, you'll want to check to make sure that hospice is covered though your policy. You can find specifics about Medicare hospice benefits on the Medicare website. You can also go to the National Hospice and Palliative Care Organization website for more information.

In a nutshell, hospice exists because it is good for everyone. It's a cost saver for the Medicare program and for insurance companies, because it results in fewer hospital admissions. And for families, it preserves the ability of the patient to stay in a comfortable, familiar environment, with a team they know (and who knows them), with all the care they need.

It's also worth noting that hospices vary in structure, rules, and quality from state to state. In some states, non-profit agencies are more prevalent. In others, hospice is a for-profit medical model, and care varies company by company. Bottom line: not every hospice is the same. Because hospice is a Medicare benefit carve out, though, you can choose the one you want, and you can change your team if you are not satisfied with the way things are being done. The best way to make sure you get a team you feel confident about from the start is to interview several in advance of when they will be needed. Ask your friends and your doctor, and even your social media network about their experiences with local hospices and which one is the best in your area.

Having worked with hospice for more than ten years, I can tell you with confidence that, overwhelmingly, the nurses, aides, doctors, and chaplains (e.g., the actual team in your home) who do this job do it because they feel a strong calling to be of service in this specific kind of work. They give because it is who they are. And they are often the best in the healthcare business.

When the time comes for hospice to arrive in your home, do yourself a favor and embrace them. Ask for hospice and ask early. They will lighten your load and when you have the right team in place, your loved one will be able to relax and feel confident that they will be well cared for and their pain will be eased.

Honestly, I can't imagine going through losing a loved one without hospice's expert and dedicated care and support. And you shouldn't have to either.

When to Call Hospice and What to Expect

It's one thing to know that hospice will need to be brought in at some point, but how do you know when that time has arrived?

Hospice is meant to be called in when your spouse is within six months of death. Realistically, no one knows exactly when a terminally ill patient will die. Your doctor and their nurses are skilled at assessing how much time a person may have, but they will be relying on you, the primary caregiver, to keep them informed of changes that point to a decline that warrants bringing hospice in.

So, what should you be looking for as the primary caregiver? The most visible sign in your loved one that they are losing ground is a marked increase in exhaustion. Other signs may include changes in appetite, shortness of breath even without exertion, and your loved one suddenly wanting to discuss end of life issues—wills, money, kids, plans. You may also notice them cutting activities short because the strain of doing things is too much, or declining invitations because they're concerned they won't be able to meet expectations.

Either a specialist who has seen your spouse or your primary care provider can issue the referral needed for hospice. They will likely have a preferred hospice they like to use, but you can tell them which one you want if you've already decided on one. If the doctor is reluctant or hard to reach, you can call the hospice of your choice and request a hospice evaluation, and they will call your doctor for the referral.

Once that call is made it typically takes mere hours to get a call back with an appointment (usually the same day) for a nurse to come to your home to do an evaluation. If you are at the hospital, they will come to you there and assist with the discharge planning to get your spouse home and on hospice with any needed equipment and meds ready for their arrival home, including an ambulance for transport if needed.

The hospice evaluation is a standard set of questions covering the patient's medical history and any records they've received so far. The nurse will tell you if it looks like it is appropriate for you to be signed on to hospice care and will consult the doctor for authorization. At that point you will sign consent forms, including HIPAA (make sure you're listed on this one as someone who will be making medical decisions and to whom information can be released) and the DNR or POLST. You will also be given a folder with the hospice's information. If hospice is being initiated, the nurse will also go over the following with you:

- What meds they are ordering
- What meds will no longer be needed
- How to reach them at all hours
- The hospice team's after-hours system
- What durable medical equipment (DME) will be coming (i.e., hospital bed, over the

bed table, oxygen concentrator and tanks, wheelchairs, walkers, fall mats, shower chair or tub seat, bedside commode or toilet riser with handles and a back, etc.)
- When meds will be delivered
- Specific instructions regarding feeding, bathing, and other care

Finally, you'll be given the names of everyone on your team (more about this team in the section to follow). They'll also need the name of the mortuary you'll be using, so that they can make that call when the time comes, so that you don't have to.

Within a few days you will have met the rest of your team, answered their initial questions, and determined what you need from them. Alternately, if services are determined to be needed right now, then by the end of the evaluation appointment, you will have an information folder, a DNR, a list of team members, and a schedule of deliveries. Afterwards, you may feel a bit stunned, struggling to absorb what has just happened. It's normal to feel bewildered or drained after such a difficult conversation. Take a breath. Let things sink in. Practice good self-care. If you can, take this moment to be with each other.

The cavalry is on its way . . .

Who's Who in Hospice Care

I've said it before, and I'll say it again: those who work in hospice do so not because it's not a job, but because it's a *calling*. Staff at these organizations believe in a few core principles that form the basis of care provided by any hospice. These include:

- That terminally ill patients deserve to die in the living situation of their choice in dignity and as comfortably as possible.
- That they should be able to do the things they want to for as long as they can.
- That they should have care at home, and should not have to spend any more time sitting or waiting in a doctor's office.
- And finally, that they should have education available to help their families understand what they are seeing and experiencing.

Hospice teams work day and night, around the clock. They become part of your family during the time they're with you, doing their best to reduce your workload (physically and emotionally). And they consider being there for your spouse's death a gift, not a job. Yes, they are professionals, and they need days off. They are only human. They think on their feet, find solutions outside a medical facility, and work as a team. They look for updates in the morning to know what occurred overnight and on weekends. They rarely have a holiday off.

Before they arrive on your doorstep, it's a good idea to have a basic understanding of what each person on the team does. That way you know what to expect from each one of them.

Social Worker

In a hospice setting, the social worker's role is to help families as they face the impact of terminal illness. In a nutshell, they handle everything except medical care. Any questions, fears, concerns, or misconceptions you may have about your loved one's illness and death can be addressed by your social worker. Other things they are there to do include:

- Acting as a go-between for family members to help enforce boundaries with visitors
- Working with children to help them say goodbye to a family member
- Talking with families about final arrangements, such as funerals or memorials, burial or cremation, etc.

In hospice, social workers are available, but not required, so be sure to ask for one if you need the assistance they can provide.

Chaplain

A chaplain is someone who provides emotional and/or spiritual support and guidance for you, your spouse, and your family. They may come from a specific religious background or be completely non-denominational, or even not any type of minster at all. When Linda met our hospice chaplain, she told her that she did not want to be prayed over. Having become more isolated because she was house bound, she just wanted an extra friend she could talk to who wouldn't panic she was tired or became short of breath. They started their own private book club for two and met weekly.

In a nutshell, your chaplain is someone prepared to sit with you and your family—including your kids—and just be there to listen and offer comfort and support in whatever way works best for your family. It can involve matters of faith or not; that's totally up to you. Or, if you prefer not to have a chaplain, you can opt out of having this person on your team. (In which case, if you change your mind later, it's never too late to ask them to step in.)

Nurse

Hospice nurses are, in my opinion, the very best of the best in a tough profession. Because they work out in the field instead of in a hospital, they have to know every disease, every symptom, every medication, every side effect, and every possible scenario. When a patient is in distress, they do what is needed and discuss it with the doctor ASAP. In addition to providing hands-on medical care, the nurse's responsibilities include:

- Advocating for patients, including asking you to allow the social worker in if they see a need not being met
- Getting you any extra help that is needed
- Knowing the laws to ensure they are not being asked to go beyond their scope of practice
- Staying on top of orders for meds, DME, and staffing, and making sure these orders are executed in a timely fashion
- Keeping meticulous notes so anyone on-call stays current on care and meds needed, along with any changes
- Making every patient and family feel that they are the only concern for that nurse in that moment.
- Being your doctor's eyes and ears on the ground

Your nurse will also prepare you for your spouse's death. Trust them. Listen to them. Ask them any questions you have. Perhaps most importantly, allow them time to establish a relationship with your spouse. Your partner needs to be able to put their trust in this person to take care of them.

Doctor

Hospice doctors are a unique group. Some are certi-fied as hospice physicians, and others are specialists in the illnesses that typically end with hospice: oncologists, pulmonologists, and others. These doctors are almost always dedicated to ensuring that the patients they saw were pain free, comfortable, and informed.

Pain and other symptoms are not always completely manageable. But if any group of physicians knows how to aggressively address pain, agitation, shortness of breath—these are the ones. When a hospice doctor visits, you are guaranteed that you will know the truth as they see it, and that you will be heard. Your concerns will be answered.

You will not see the doctor frequently, but you will experience them coming to your home for appointments and taking time to answer your questions. Their goal is to get ahead of the symptoms and to stay ahead of them. And for this, they will stay in contact with your nurse so that they are made aware of any changes that occur. The standard of care for hospice includes that there is a team meeting in their office at least every other week to discuss your spouse's current needs.

For your doctor to do their best work, give them space to do their job. Let them get to know your spouse and their needs. Keep your journal of concerns handy so you don't forget to ask questions and air concerns. And please, don't be afraid of the meds they're using. They know what they're doing. Your spouse is at the end of their life, and the goal is comfort above all else.

Most doctors do not volunteer to work out of their cars, covering multiple areas, and being available around the clock. It takes a special doctor to work in hospice. They tell it like it is, and they take care of business.

The Hands that Help

Hospice is clearly a special organization for me, personally. I worked in hospice. I have had hospice in my home twice. And I have seen hospice help ease suffering and strain in the homes of many friends too. My bias aside, hospice will give you and your spouse a team who have just one goal: a peaceful death following the very best quality of life they can provide.

To get the ball rolling, you will have to face paper-work and be okay with visitors in your home. In exchange, you will have care available around the clock, education about what to expect, and the support you need while your spouse is dying.

To get started with hospice, ask your doctor in advance what hospices they refer out to. Ask your social circle which hospices they have used or heard about. Take the time to check out these referred organizations. Ask every one of them if they have continuous-care-dedicated staff. Ask how their on-call system works, and about frequency of visits. Go with the one that you and your spouse feel the most confident in and comfortable with. Then, as your spouse's illness progresses, ask the doctor when it will be time.

Remember, hospice is for the last six months of life—not the last six days or six hours. Starting earlier is legal and will provide the support that you and your spouse will need. This will reduce your fatigue and stress. You will know your team well before the end, which means you'll be able to relax a bit and trust them. Hospice is there for you, but only if you *allow* them to be. Do that for yourself, for your spouse, and for your family. You won't be sorry you did. You're much more likely to wonder how you ever got along before without them.

At this point, you're as prepared as anyone can be for what's to come. Even so, no one is ever truly ready for the day their spouse takes their final breath. In the next chapter, we'll talk about saying goodbye when that day comes. Closure is important for everyone involved here, and we're going to do our best to make sure everyone that who needs it gets it.

6

SAYING GOODBYE

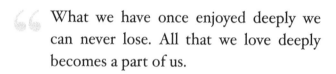What we have once enjoyed deeply we can never lose. All that we love deeply becomes a part of us.

— Helen Keller

Till Death Do Us Part

At this point in your journey, you have walked through the steps of preparation for what's about to happen. The moment is drawing close. It's time to say goodbye.

So many times in my professional life I've heard someone tell me they just can't bring themselves to say the words. They can't tell their loved one it's okay for them to go. Helping your spouse transition is your final gift to them. It's also one of the very hardest things you will ever do. Even so, there is a certain sacredness to sitting with someone as they fade from this life.

In this chapter I'm going to cover everything you need to know but never wanted to about this difficult but also potentially beautiful and unforgettable time in your lives. First, we'll cover how to say goodbye in a way that promotes healing for both you and your spouse. Then I'll educate you about the dying process itself. This will include a rundown of what happens to the body when death is imminent and actually occurring. This is an uncomfortable topic, to be sure, but if you know what to expect, you can focus on being present for and with your spouse in their final moments. The risk of not having this knowledge is needless worry and upset on your part during an already impossibly difficult time.

Finally, we'll go over what happens in the minutes, hours, and first few days after a death—from preparing the body for transit to making arrangements and planning the funeral. This knowledge will not be easy to take in, but it will empower you and make your recovery easier. And it will allow you to fully be there for your spouse during the last moments you have together on this earth. That is an incredibly precious gift for both of you.

And one you'll be so grateful for in the months and years that follow.

A Time to Let Go

It has finally come: the moment you'll say goodbye to the person you love. The pain most of us feel in this moment is unimaginable to many who haven't yet walked in our shoes. But like any other pain we face in life, it's up to us how we will bear it.

When it arrives, there is no escaping this moment. It's coming whether you're ready or not, so for your own sake and your spouse's, you had best be as ready as you can be for it. That is really at the crux of all the work you've been doing so far along this journey, after all—to minimize suffering and maximize the value of the time you've got left.

Like the other challenges you've faced so far, the best way to deal with this one is to get out ahead of it. Figure out what you and your spouse need out of this goodbye and do you darndest to give that to yourself and each other.

Envision what you want those final moments to be like. Is there anyone who should be there with you? Is there anyone either of you specifically *do not* want there who might feel they are entitled to be? If so, stand your ground. It's not anyone else's place to say who gets to be there except yours and your spouse's. Will you want a beloved pet there? Or music that will be comforting to both of you?

Figure out what you both want and make your wishes known to any others involved. Make sure that any preparations needed are taken care of well in advance.

You will also need to think about whether there's anything you still need to say to your spouse before they leave this world, in those final moments. This can be especially difficult. What is it you want your spouse to know before they leave this life? It can help to think about what words you would want to hear as you faded from this world. If you need to practice what to say with a trusted friend or a therapist, that's okay. Journaling can also help.

You have the opportunity to tell your spouse, one last time, that you will never forget them. They will live on in you, and you will keep their memory alive. You can thank them for your time together, for the special moments engraved in your heart. And even if you can't tell them it's okay for them to go, you *can* tell them that you will always love them, always hold them close, and that you will be okay with the support you have around you.

Fearing that the spouse you're leaving behind will *not* be okay afterwards is one of the most common fears faced by a dying person, so setting your loved one's mind at ease about this is one of the greatest gifts you can give them.

Though you may not realize it at the time, it's also a gift to yourself. It's is likely the first time you will say—with confidence through the tears—that you will indeed get through this.

And you will. Saying it out loud for the first time will help you to believe that this is truly possible.

The Death Process: What to Expect

As you prepare to become a surviving spouse, I urge you to educate yourself about the process the body actually goes through leading up to and during death. This section may be difficult to read, but it will serve to demystify what can otherwise be a very frightening thing to witness if you're not prepared for it—especially when you are watching someone you love go through it. This knowledge will give you the confidence and steadiness you need to truly be there for your spouse when they have never needed you more.

We'll go over some specific physical and mental symptoms and signifiers of death below, but it's important to understand some general facts about the dying process before we get to these. To start with, this process can be fast or slow, and can even progress in spurts. It may begin suddenly or may seem a long time in coming. Each death progresses in its own time, as unique as the individual experiencing it.

Some people seem to have an innate understanding of what's happening to them when their death is imminent, though they may not be able (or want) to articulate this. Be sure to pay attention to any unusual signals they send.

Linda gave me a sign like this when her time came. For months toward the end of her illness, she had disdained the hospital bed I'd set up for her in the living room, next to our big bay window overlooking the garden, refusing to even look at it. But on a Friday afternoon during the last week she was alive, she said, "I think I am going to try this today." Once she climbed into it, she never went upstairs to our bedroom again. She felt what was coming, and this was her way of letting me know it was time.

Signs that Death is Approaching Soon

Some things to look for that signal death is approaching can include:

- **Appetite changes, specifically lack of hunger**
- A dying person's body no longer needs nutrition and systems are beginning to shut down. This is simply the body's natural wisdom that eating is no longer necessary.
- **Loss of sense of thirst**
- When the body is no longer utilizing fluids and the kidneys have stopped processing them, thirst signals are no longer sent. In fact, at this point, forcing fluids with an IV drip will flood the body with unnecessary fluids that it does not need and is not prepared to deal with, which is likely to make the patient feel much worse rather than better.
- **Fever**

- As the body shuts down and stops filtering blood, fever naturally occurs. Provide cooling measures for comfort, but greater intervention is not needed at this point.
- **Loss of energy and sleeping more**
- Once the body begins to truly shut down, the patient experiences a sudden and drastic loss of energy. It's normal for a dying person to sleep for most of the day at this point. They may drift in and out of consciousness or even a coma state.
- **Breathing changes**
- Within hours or minutes of death, the brain stops sending messages to breathe regularly, and even to swallow, resulting in noisy breaths that sound worse than they actually are. You're hearing a little fluid on the vocal cords and in the windpipe is all. Linda's death involved about four hours of this. Casper spent the last week of her life breathing as little as three times a minute sometimes.

Remember: as alarming as these signs can appear to be, these are all normal, natural signs of the processes the body goes through as death nears. It's important that others in your home who may serve as caretakers for your spouse are made familiar with these signs too, so they know what to look for. Make sure they know you want to be kept informed if they should notice any of these things.

What Happens to the Body During Death

When death is actively occurring, the signs are almost universal. During the death process, the following changes occur:

- **Breathing changes**
- Irregular breathing (known as Chaines-Stokes) with long stretches of no respiration followed by regular, rapid, or slow breathing are common. This can be hard to watch because it looks uncomfortable, like gasping. Rest assured that the patient is unaware of what's happening. Your spouse is not suffocating.
- **Gurgling in the throat, especially during breathing**
- This is caused by fluid not being swallowed and landing on the back of the throat. Again, the patient is unaware this is occurring; this is not a sign of drowning or discomfort. This is also frequently mistaken as a "death rattle," but does not indicate death is occurring at precisely this moment.
- **Uneven temperatures around the body**
- This occurs when the hypothalamus stops regulating body temperature.
- **Inability to process food or pills**
- At this stage, the GI system has shut

down. Any food or pills introduced will not be absorbed, and if swallowing has ceased, they will not go down at all.

- **<u>Cooling and mottling in the limbs</u>**
- As the heart stops circulating blood and draws the blood supply to the heart and brain, mottling makes the limbs look purplish.
- **<u>Swelling of the fingers</u>**
- As blood stops circulating it pools in the body. If your spouse is wearing any rings, it's time to take them off now, gently but quickly. Use soap or oil if necessary.
- **<u>Incontinence</u>**
- **<u>Inability to speak</u>**
- **<u>Loss of eye focus</u>**
- **<u>Heart rate and blood pressure drop</u>**
- The heart rate slows and blood pressure falls. At some point it will not be possible to take blood pressure any longer. The heart rate drops off altogether at the very end.
- Eventually, the breathing will slow and finally cease.
- A dying person can hear you talk until their last breath, and often for up to a few moments after. Keep talking to them. Hold their hand. Provide a sense of comfort as you know they would want it.
- A dying person may not die with their eyes

closed. And unlike what we see in the movies, the eyes and mouth often do not stay shut after death.

Your hospice, once they enter the picture, should also go over these signs with you and are a wonderful resource to tap if you have additional questions or concerns about what to expect. They can also leave literature behind to assist you as well as any other caretakers or visitors in understanding what will happen during this time.

What Happens Afterwards?

In the first moments after your spouse dies, the nurse or other hospice staff will pronounce the death and then determine the time of death and record it. Next, they will probably leave the room to notify their agency and the coroner's office, which allows the release of your spouse's remains to the mortuary. They will also call the mortuary for you to notify them.

So, what do you do now? You have spent the last weeks or months, or maybe even years focusing on taking care of your ailing spouse. That job now belongs to the mortuary. Your job is to be a recently bereaved widow or widower.

But how do you do that? This moment in your life may feel like a huge vacuum has opened under your feet. You expected it. You knew it was coming. But now it's here, and it's easy to feel overwhelmed, especially in the grip of fresh, immediate grief.

In my experience, the main thing you're going to need in this moment is a little *time*. Only time will allow you to process what has just happened. And that means arranging things beforehand so that the people you know you can rely on can step in and manage any and all of your responsibilities so that you can take the time you need right now for yourself.

It is unreasonable for you or anyone else to expect you to be able to focus—or really, even to function—for the next few hours. This includes the inability to function as a parent right now. In a previous chapter, we covered the importance of assigning one adult to each individual child, someone they know, trust, and feel comfortable with. That adult is going to be responsible for keeping eyes on that child and tending to their needs during this time *so you do not have to supervise*. As much as you will want to, you will not be able to tend to them right now the way that they need. The kids may not even need to know this has been arranged. As long as it's someone they are close to and trust (and who you trust to do this), it will be okay.

Pets may need to be put somewhere so they don't become aggressive with the mortuary staff upon arrival. If the pet was close to your spouse, please remember that they grieve and need to say goodbye too. Allow them to see and approach your spouse so they understand what has occurred. Make sure that there is something set aside for pets—a blanket from the bed, or clothing that smells like your spouse— to allow them to keep the scent for later.

Kids should see the spouse after death has occurred too, so they can fully process what has happened. If both kids and pets are involved, involving the pet in this process with the children can help normalize the experience for them and provide comfort. You may want to wait until after your spouse has been bathed post-mortem for this final visit.

Notably, the kids aren't the only ones who need someone to be able to focus on and be there for them during this time. Ask someone you trust and who will be able to hold it together during this time to keep an eye on *you*. This person should make ensure you stay hydrated, have a little bite to eat as needed, and are not saddled with demands or expectations from other people right now.

This is a surreal time, but one of the things that can help you get through it is keeping in mind what you've just done for your spouse: your job as a loving partner, fulfilling the vows you swore the day you got married. You have walked them through their final moments, just as you promised you would.

Final Arrangements

After the death of your spouse has occurred, a few things need to happen. As always, our goal here is to get as much as possible of this done *before* today so that there are as few demands on you as possible in the immediate aftermath.

None of this is an emergency. These are just things that must be taken care of.

First, the coroner will release your spouse's remains (typically by phone) to be turned over to the mortuary, at which point the mortuary must be notified. As previously mentioned, hospice should handle both of these tasks for you.

You may choose to bathe your spouse's body and dress them in clothing you have laid aside. If you want the hospice staff or friends to do that for you or with you that is your decision. Remember that and prepare for it. Speak up- and remember that all of this is optional. You can simply take your time and allow the mortuary to remove them as they died. It does not reflect badly on you if you do not do anything more than wait for the mortuary. If they are being cremated with no service the clothes your spouse leaves your home in will be what they wear. If they are going to be prepared for a service then you can take those clothes to the mortuary later and the staff there will dress them and prepare them. Some faiths require that people of that faith dress and prepare the body and the mortuary will facilitate that. (It is important to know that sometimes after death the clothing that is left on the body will become soiled or become difficult to remove, so returning those items is not something to expect).

When the mortuary staff arrives, you will be

asked to step out while they transfer your spouse to their cot. Once that is done, you can choose to follow them out or to remain inside. Again, it's up to you and what you need in that moment. Note, though, that if you are doing a direct cremation this will be your very last time to see your spouse's face in person.

There will also be the need to communicate news of the death to your family, friends, and community. I recommend making a list ahead of time of who needs to be notified and assigning a friend or family member to make these calls for you when the time comes. Likewise, if you have specific requests about what should or should not be shared on social media, make sure that the person making these calls knows this in advance so they can relay your wishes. Feel free to impose limits on visits, expectations to return calls, and other social obligations at this time depending on what you need to be okay. If there are any calls you need to make personally, find a quiet space where you will not be interrupted.

Note that there is one other call you may be facing personally. If your spouse was an organ donor or you live in an automatic donor state, you will receive a call from your local donor bank, usually about an hour or so after your spouse's death. The call to the coroner triggers this, and if you're not prepared for it, it can be extremely upsetting. Make sure you know in advance what your spouse's wishes are regarding these donations.

Understand that if you say 'yes' to donation, you

will be asked about your spouse's sexual history, medical history, drug history, and more during this phone call, for the safety of anyone who will be receiving tissue from the body. If the donor bank can use specific organs (that includes skin, bone, and other tissue) they legally have to tell you, in detail, how this will happen so you can verbally consent. Time is of the essence for these donations, and I get that, but this can be a particularly horrific call to receive and have to get through when you are raw and hurting from your loss. Should you consent, also be aware that skin and bone donation can *possibly* impact an open casket service.

You will also be asked if you will allow your spouse's donations to be used just for research, or for sale to medical facilities. Think that through how you feel about this ahead of time, preferably together, so you don't have to decide in the moment, alone. If you are donating your spouse's body to science, check the reputation of the donation service well ahead of time, and be aware you will be asked if their remains can be used for military or law enforcement purposes. While such donations are valuable for keeping our service members and law enforcement officers educated and safe, you may find some of the ways that donated bodies are used here to be objectionable. Educate yourself and make an informed decision.

Donation is a precious gift, but it has consequences for you depending on your beliefs and what kind of service you want. So be sure to take all of this into consideration in advance.

The Funeral

You have one last major task as a recently bereaved widow: planning and getting through the funeral or memorial service. This is a lot to manage, but I strongly recommend that you take it on as your own. No one knew your spouse better than you, so there's no one better to make sure that the ceremony celebrating their life is one that is worthy of them. This is not to say you should be doing everything yourself —far from it. But you should certainly take a managing role in the process. Doing this will help you get organized and feel back in control of your life again—which, take it from me, is *huge* right now.

There's another good reason to handle this yourself. In arranging this celebration of the person you love, this is where you are going to establish how you will handle your grief and recovery process. Make it what you want for your spouse.

Eulogizing Your Spouse

I gave the eulogy for both of my spouses. If that is your choice, the words you use in your eulogy are yours alone. I chose to do the eulogy so I could let the world know how my spouse was to be remembered. If that's yours as well, be honest about what they were like. No one is perfect, including them, and it's a disservice to them and to all those grieving for them right now to pretend otherwise. Speak of how you will keep their memory alive in the future. Be cautious about statements that include never loving again, not feeling like you can get through this, or anything else that will set you up for expectations that are not realistic or healthy for your future.

Choosing Speakers

If others are to speak, choose *who* will speak carefully. If you have kids, allow them to participate, but don't make this mandatory. Most importantly, allow kids to back out even during the service if they are not up to it. It's okay either way. Really, it is. Make sure they know that. If they think they will want to say something, let them write it (or help them to do so) in their own words.

You don't have to allow anyone to speak if you're not comfortable with them doing so. You do not have to offer an open mic. The entire service is yours to plan. It can be somber if that is how you see it or need it to be, or it can be a celebration if that is more your style. You get to set the tone.

Type of Reception

If you wish, after the formal service (if you have one), you can have a more informal reception at the mortuary, a church or temple, or wherever else the service is (following the rules of the venue, of course), or you can do this at home, or both.

For Casper, I had a reception at church with all

the things she loved and that we shared together: her favorite candy bar, Hawaiian flowers and shave ice, and a simple catered meal to cut down on the amount of work I had to do.

For Linda's funeral, after the church reception, I chose to have a second gathering at home. I heated the pool for the kids and their friends, and created a relaxed environment for myself and the people who were truly supportive during Linda's illness and her passing. After a crazy week of planning and busy-work, this finally gave me a chance to sit and relax surrounded by people I loved and who loved me—and who all loved Linda too. That meant the world to me.

When the Funeral Is Over

In our society, bereavement is expected to begin and end in the blink of an eye. Most employers provide only three days of leave time for a significant death. Polls suggest that most Americans think it should take less than a month before the primary griever "returns to normal." These expectations and provisions are not terribly realistic.

After the funeral, everyone else goes back to real life. Yes, they lost someone too, but if they are not the ones going home to a house where the person who died lived, it is not a moment-to-moment loss.

For primary grievers, we are grappling with that loss constantly in the first days and weeks following a death. We go to the grocery store and are painfully aware we don't have that person to shop for. We wake up and have to remember they are dead. We have a special moment or a difficult one and we reach for the phone—and they are not there. Even social media reminds us with daily memories. Initial grief can be stunning and incredibly disjointing. Each day or moment becomes a comparison of how long it has been since they died, how different it is now than it was before.

As a new widow, it is up to you to ensure you are taking care of yourself, not expecting too much of yourself, and not allowing *others* to determine what you will do or when you will do it. The process of adapting and recovering starts now, with you setting limits to meet your needs. In the first few days that might mean simply being able to adapt to the first realization in the morning that your spouse is dead. Getting up at some point. Getting dressed. Dealing with a few daily life responsibilities. You will find your way. Set your boundaries and hang on. The work you've done up to this point will get you through this.

This concludes the first part of your journey as a Rebellious Widow and the first half of this book. In the second part, we'll examine the existing paradigm of what we're taught grief looks like and come to understand how, for primary caregiver spouses who lose their partner to a terminal illness, this paradigm is surprisingly ill-fitting. We'll also take a deeper look at the Widow Rules and unmask them for what they are: cruel nonsense. Armed with this understanding, you'll be prepared to process your grief and to heal from it in a way that is better and healthier for you. And to begin to look ahead to the possibilities life still holds for you as you continue moving forward.

It doesn't feel like it at first, but life does go on. And you deserve to find peace and happiness in it.

7

REWRITING THE GRIEF PARADIGM

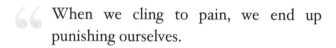 When we cling to pain, we end up
punishing ourselves.

— LEO BUSCAGLIA

A Window Opens

U p to this point, we've been talking about how
to cope with what is coming. Starting here,
though, we're moving into new territory: what
happens *after*. After your partner has died. After
you've laid them to rest. After you've had a few days
or weeks to absorb and begin to process everything
that has happened. It's my hope that at this point in
the journey, what you've learned so far in the pages of
this book have brought you some measure of solace
and comfort. Now it's time to take that new knowledge and apply it to what comes next.

For so long, you've been focused on helping your partner prepare for their death. Now the focus shifts to you, their survivor. This second half of the book is tailored to helping you learn to manage this strange new territory you find yourself in, and to successfully navigate what remains of the grieving process.

Transitioning from the anticipatory grief you've known up until now to what you will feel after your partner's death is a big shift. The task that lies before you here is coping with this new grief. The goal is to do so in a healthy way that leads to recovering from grief and remaking your life. And unfortunately for us, popular conceptions about what grief is and how it works—even the one used by professional counselors and therapists—are not always all that helpful. In fact, because the existing grief framework is so limited, linear, and restrictive, it can actually make our grieving process *more* difficult and stressful, because all too often the reality of grief we experience doesn't fit into all those nice, neat little boxes.

In this chapter, we'll take a closer look at the current paradigm of the "stages" of grief and break down how these are thought to work versus what you might actually experience. We'll also do some work together to demystify this narrative of grief to help normalize the reality of grieving so you don't have to worry you're "doing it wrong," as so many people have before you. Finally, I'll introduce you to a new framework for how to think about grieving that I've found more useful both for myself and in my work as a professional grief counselor, particularly for Rebellious Widows.

First up, let's take a hard look at the way we're told or expected to process grief, versus how this actually plays out person to person.

The Problem with the Five Stages

I'll be up front in saying that I'm not a fan of the traditional grief paradigm. Viewing grief as occurring in clear-cut stages actually creates stress for grievers. I can't tell you how many times I have had new clients come in for grief work concerned because they have not reached anger yet. Or they are not yet at bargaining. Or they felt better and now they are having a tough day and it feels like they are in some kind of weird grief relapse and are "failing" at grieving.

This is the trouble with the mainstream framework of how grief works: not everyone's experience looks the same or fits the same pattern. So, when we're told there's only one way to do it "right" in order to reach a place of acceptance and healing, that makes things *harder* for us, not easier.

This isn't to say that there aren't useful things you can take from the groundbreaking work of Dr. Elisabeth Kubler-Ross. Her stages of grief work best when they are used as a means of understanding what a dying person might face in their emotional journey toward acceptance. This grief framework got us talking about death and dying, helping our culture to break long-held taboos about even speaking the word death. However, she didn't intend for her stages to be seen as linear and mandatory. Rather, the stages were just a way to conceptualize the dying process so people could finally begin to understand it during a time when talking about this topic, even in private, even *while or after it had occurred*, was considered unseemly.

Kubler-Ross's stages were the first cultural step in making grief—or anticipatory grief, at least— something we could understand and talk about. Over time, however, we really haven't gone back and looked at where they began and why they were a necessary step in what should have continued to be an evolving framework for understanding *what grief is* in all its varied forms and *how it works*. Instead, as the seminal work on the subject, the stages simply became what we "know" about grief—a stopping point, for many, instead of a beginning. One of the downsides of this is that this model can be counterproductive for those of us grieving a death after the fact rather than before, especially if we've had months or years to come to terms with that death before it occurred.

We are all better for Kubler-Ross's work because it started a crucial cultural conversation about death and began to normalize these discussions in a healthy way. She gave us the underpinnings of a language we can use to talk about death and grief that is still useful so long as we don't think about these stages too rigidly.

Before we get to discussing the new grief

paradigm I'm going to introduce you to here, I think it's valuable to briefly go over the traditional five stages of grief. Understanding the existing paradigm will give you important context for why our new one is needed.

The Five Stages of Grief... and Why They May or May Not Apply to You

As defined by Dr. Kubler-Ross, the five stages of grief are: denial, anger, bargaining, depression, and acceptance. She utilized those terms to describe the experience of a dying person in such a way that they and their families could understand what they were likely to feel. These stages have since been used almost universally by clinicians and society at large to apply labels to grief, and to seemingly instruct grievers about what they *should* experience.

In fact, many clinicians and society at large continue to think that experiencing all of these stages is required, in that order, or that you will never be completely ready for "acceptance." I hear it in my office, and I hear it in presentations to large audiences of clinicians. When I ask what people—even audiences made up of professionals in counseling and psychology—know about grief, they go straight to the stages. New clients come in saying they are "doing grief wrong" because they have not experienced one stage or another.

In truth, some of these stages do not apply to many grievers. This is often particularly the case if you had a long time during your spouse's terminal illness to prepare yourself for what was coming. In cases like these, thinking you are *supposed to* experience and go through each of these emotional stages can actually get in the way of a grieving spouse's ability to process and cope.

In addition to being particularly useful to people who learn they are going to die of a terminal illness upon diagnosis, the framework of the stages can also assist those who have experienced the sudden death of a loved one. But even then they do not fit perfectly in every case, and they do not describe anything related to healing at the end, much less an exact path for how to get there.

Below, I'm going to break down each of the five "stages" of grief so that we can understand them and how they may—or may not—play into our individual processes of grieving.

Denial

In this context, denial is the mindset that death will not actually happen despite evidence to the contrary. A person told that they are dying by their doctors thinks, "No, I am not really going to die."

The long and short of it is that denial is a coping mechanism. Its purpose is to give you time to sort out how you will assimilate this new information so that you can begin to actually deal with it. When you first get the news that your spouse is sick, denial is a perfectly reasonable initial response for either or both of you. But after months or years of coping with a spouse's terminal illness, denial is not something a widow is likely to experience once their spouse passes away.

You may, however, hold onto a sense that this cannot be real. You may even do so for a long time, wishing fervently for just one more day with your spouse. What you are experiencing in those moments is not necessarily denial, but a natural part of transitioning into the next part of your life and wishing this transition was not necessary.

Anger

Under the old paradigm of the five stages, the second stage is being angry that you or someone you love is going to die, or did die. As a spouse grieving after what may have been the long illness of your partner, you may indeed feel angry. But is it *necessary* to feel angry? No.

For the purposes of a Rebellious Widow, anger often represents the unfinished business of loss—all the things you did not get to say or do or show, or conversations or experiences you wanted but did not get to have. This may include conflicts you buried, either because that's how your marriage worked or because you didn't feel it was appropriate to be angry with a spouse who was dying. Some of you, however, will never experience anger. You may have a different set of coping skills, or you may have just had a relationship where you always dealt with things as they came up and then finished them.

If you are feeling angry, the key thing to do for yourself and your healing is to determine what it is you're angry about. Was there something you didn't get to do or say before they died? Or something you discovered since their death that might have caused hurt? Once you know the source of your anger, you can deal with it in whatever way works best for you. Writing about it (perhaps in letter form) or talking it out with someone you trust can work wonders.

The important part, if you are experiencing anger, is to acknowledge and express it in a healthy way so it can't hold you back from recovering and healing.

Bargaining

Bargaining, or trying to cut some kind miracle deal with a higher power (God, the medical establishment, etc.) to save the life of the person you love, often occurs soon after a diagnosis is learned or when someone is actually dying. My favorite example of bargaining occurred as a friend in our church was dying. Mari was the life of our kids' programs, and an entire generation grew up with her in Sunday school and on youth trips. Then, suddenly, she was dying of cancer. The church kids had to be told so they could prepare to say goodbye. My niece and nephew were in Sunday School when the adults broke this news. There were tears, happy memories shared, anger at God for allowing Mari, of all people, to be so sick that she would die. Then came bargaining. A little hand went up, following by a question. "Can we give God my grandma and keep Mari? Grandma has already had a long time."

For the loss of a spouse, bargaining occurs between diagnosis and death, including frantic searches for cures, promising greater devotion to God if your spouse could stay alive, and all manner of other efforts to stop them from dying. Bargaining after the death of a spouse following a long illness, however, is incredibly unlikely. You know your spouse has died and that not a single thing will change if you try bargaining for their return. So, don't be surprised or concerned if you skip this altogether after your spouse's death has occurred.

Depression

I'm not going to beat around the bush here. The fact that one of these stages is labeled "depression" is highly problematic and can be extremely confusing for many people. Real depression is a mental health issue with specific diagnostic criteria. It's important to understand that grievers are not experiencing mental illness just because they are grieving. If they have a history of it beforehand, then depression should certainly be watched for. Grief involves *sadness*, not necessarily depression. They are not the same thing. For all of these reasons, it's vitally important to reframe this aspect of your recovery as *sadness*, not as depression—unless, of course, you have been clinically diagnosed with depression beforehand or during this time.

Regardless of whether it occurs before or after the actual death, the sadness that comes with grief can be so intense that it feels like it is going to rip you apart. That is not depression. It's a perfectly normal and sane reaction to having such a vitally important person taken from your life, especially in the initial weeks after their death. There will be sadness. It will come and go, and it will lessen as you feel your way through it, finish your grief, and reintegrate into your new life.

It's also important to note that, while depression is not synonymous with grief, if you have a history of major depression or bipolar disorder, the loss of a spouse can be especially devastating, and can cause a depressive episode. If you have a history of clinical depression, let your healthcare provider know your spouse is dying or has died, and that you might need to be seen or have medications adjusted to help you adapt to your new normal.

Acceptance

Traditionally, acceptance is where a dying person finally believes and acknowledges that they are going to die and becomes ready to say goodbye. Grievers almost universally respond with anger when they are told they need to reach a state of "acceptance" that their spouse or loved one has died. They know their spouse died—after all, they are the one waking up to their new reality. Being told that you need to reach acceptance can feel like being told a combination of "get over it" and "time to move on." As a result, this can be a highly problematic stage to expect a surviving spouse to experience after their late spouse's long illness. The same can go for anyone who has lost a loved one after having been up close and personal with their long-term illness and death.

As I mentioned before, you, your spouse, and your other close loved ones may experience some, none, or all of these stages of grief, and if they do show up, they may do so "out of order." When grief rears its head, give yourself time to cope. Be kind to yourselves, and practice good self-care.

Next up, let's look more closely at how grief can affect our ability to function day to day.

The Effects of Grief

When grief hits, it can do so with such sudden and intense force that it sometimes feels like a tidal wave or an earthquake. It impacts our energy level and our ability to function in our daily lives, and can be very disruptive.

Below, I'll break down the cognitive, physical, and emotional toll that grief can take on a person. Once you know what to be on guard against, you can make any arrangements you need at this time to help yourself stay on track to remain healthy so you'll have the energy to pursue your recovery.

Cognitive

In grief, your thinking is processed through a brain that feels surrounded by cotton batting. Thoughts are slower, decisions harder, and your ability to focus and concentrate will come and go. Confusion is common and can lead to memory lapses, poor decision-making, becoming easily frustrated, and having very little energy for extending empathy toward others. That last one is especially difficult for caregivers, because we are accustomed to helping everyone, and suddenly we just don't have that in us anymore.

All of this is normal and to be expected. You can get ready by putting your bills on autopay, any income on automatic deposit and, most importantly, by giving yourself permission to not give of yourself as much as you are used to giving for the time being. It's okay to just take a break.

Tell those needing support that you sympathize with them, and you hope they have a support system to help because right now you cannot be that for them at this time. Even driving can be incredibly dangerous when you cannot concentrate. Use a ride service or take a cab. Do not expect yourself to remember appointments without a calendar and a reminder. Make lists of what you need to do while you're thinking about it, so you can have that information at hand without having to rely on memory.

You've got this. You just need a little more help than usual to make things easier on yourself while you focus on recovering.

Physical

Grief also takes a lot out of you physically. The main place you're likely to notice this is your energy level. The exhaustion of grief is like no other, but it will pass. Grief also causes an inflammatory response, so anything you can do to take care of your body right now is important. For starters, make sure your labs are up to date, and that you've had your annual physical and your flu shot. Caregivers are notorious for having shoulder and back injuries, headaches, and back pain. If you have these kinds of injuries or symptoms, get them addressed.

Sleep can be a real issue during this time. Many grieving people especially have trouble with staying asleep between the hours of two and five in the morning. If you find yourself sleepless at night, try to work in a nap or two during the day to make up for it. And instead of lying there in bed unable to sleep in the wee hours, if you know you're not going to sleep, get up and do something else: journal, draw, listen to music, watch some funny TV. This too shall pass.

And if you are craving carbs, indulge a little. Just add broccoli to your menu the same day you eat ice cream, and go for a walk. You don't have to be perfect. You just have to find some balance.

Emotional

The emotional impact of grief involves more than just sadness. Indeed, grief's two most common sidekicks are fear and guilt. You may also experience anger, being easily frustrated, hyperreactivity, feeling distanced from friends, or like withdrawing from those around you. It is also likely that you will experience grief attacks, moments of powerfully intense sadness that take over and then recede.

You will wish you could uninvite these new pals, but they will be walking with you on your path through to recovery. The thing is, *you* get to decide how much they will be in control, and how much you will be. My best advice here is to create reasonable expectations for yourself. You're not going to feel quite like your usual self for a while, and this is normal. Acknowledge and accept your feelings when they come up without judgement. Find a safe and productive way to express them as needed. And allow yourself space to take breaks when necessary to deal with what you're feeling. This can include taking a break from specific people if that's what you need, especially those who continue to make demands on your time and energy right now when you need to focus on your own healing.

If you are feeling guilty about anything, remember that you did the best you could. You made every decision for the right reason.

A New Grief Paradigm

As you can see, the existing paradigm of what grief is supposed to look like, while it does have some useful parts, is surprisingly limited and restrictive. We need a new way to understand how we actually process this experience—especially those of us who have lost a spouse after a long terminal illness. That's where Rebellious Widowhood comes in.

The first and most important thing to understand about this new paradigm is this: grief does not last forever. It should not be allowed to. When we lose our spouse it changes us forever, but that doesn't mean that this loss should *define* us forever. There are no stages, but there are most definitely phases, and these phases are determined by the griever, not by those around them.

Grief is where you do the emotional work still left undone at the time your loved one died. It's where you take all that once was, all that yet needs to be repaired and finished, all the good memories and the difficult ones, and recreate from all of this a reorganized life for yourself. This is your time to sort it all out, with a goal of healing and recovery.

Grief is a place for you to do this work, and when it is done, to *exit* from. It's not healthy physically or emotionally to stay there forever. Yes, you will have moments where you miss your loved one intensely. That will never change. But these moments will become fewer over time as you adapt, reorganize, and heal piece by piece.

We'll explore this new paradigm more closely in the next chapter when we break down what it means to be a Rebellious Widow. First, let's take a deeper dive into how our new grief paradigm compares to the older one, once we get up close and personal with it.

A Thought Experiment: Two Paths Through Grief

Imagine living through your grief over your spouse's death in the old paradigm. Even if you're lucky enough to be receiving counseling *not* rooted in the rigidity of the five stages, you're almost certainly still working under the understanding that you will grieve *forever*. That when you miss your late spouse on special days or have a sad moment, it means you are still grieving. Taken to its logical conclusion, grief therefore defines the rest of your entire life. From here on out, you are a grieving widow. Period.

Now let's look at the same scenario through the lens of our new paradigm. Imagine you start seeing a therapist who tells you that grief is not pathology. Rather, it is a normal response to a truly rotten experience. You hear the words "this isn't forever." You're told that you can keep your loved one with you in your new life—because this isn't about getting over them or past them or accepting they are dead. It's simply about finding a new way forward through and *out of* grief instead.

You are told it's okay to laugh, to smile, to reconfigure your life on your own time frame, when *you* are ready—not when others are. It's even okay to have sex again. And when you start reorganizing your life, you're able to set healthy boundaries so those around you respect your process, your decisions, and your right to happiness. You can remember your spouse just the way you knew them. You will include them, but don't have to feel guilty for not crying when you think or talk about them, or for retaining your capacity to feel joy, love, pleasure, excitement and all life's other positive emotions.

The difference between these two approaches to managing grief and loss are like night and day. And the second way, the Rebellious Widow way, means doing grief *your* way. Your choices. Your boundaries. Your new healthy and happy life.

And you're the only one who can give this precious gift to yourself. In the next chapter, I'll show you how.

8

BUCK THE RULES

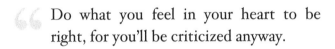 Do what you feel in your heart to be
right, for you'll be criticized anyway.

— Eleanor Roosevelt

Do It Your Way

You already know I am not fond of the rules
that society dictates for widows.

They didn't fit me when I lost Linda, nor when
Casper died. My clients in therapy consistently make
it clear that the rules don't fit them either. They are
unhealthy, unkind, and uncompromising—and that
last bit is a pretty big problem once you realize that
the rules completely contradict themselves in just
about every way possible.

The rules are exhausting, and like the stages, they
leave new widows feeling like we are doing grief

wrong. Having your intimate partner die is challenging enough. Being told you are grieving "improperly" on top of the pain of your loss makes everything so much harder. Moving away from the rules alleviates the need to try to make everyone around you happy. Say it with me here: you don't have to do grief their way. You're going to do it *your* way instead. Breaking away from the rules by deliberately and thoughtfully determining your own path through grief and into recovery is a gift that only you can give yourself.

Widowhood is not a role any of us signed up for. You didn't have a choice in losing your partner. You do, however, have a choice now. You can choose to reorganize and create a life you never considered possible in the context of that relationship. Widowhood can mean creating that new life, embracing a new outlook, and giving yourself space to make the changes you want and need for what comes next.

That is the essence of becoming a Rebellious Widow: embracing and planning for a life you didn't ask for but are determined to make the best of. You've been through something truly awful. And now that you're on the other side of it, you deserve to seize every ounce of meaning, fulfilment and joy this world holds for you.

In this chapter, we'll break down the Widow Rules and explore why they need to go. Then we'll take a closer look at what it means to adopt the new paradigm of the Rebellious Widow, and why doing so just might save your life.

The Rebellious Widow

First up, let's make sure we're starting off with a solid understanding of exactly what the widow rules are.

The Widow Rules, and Why They Need to Go

In the interest of helping you to understand the rules, identify situations in which you're being confronted with one, and cope with them, below I present a list of the widow rules. This list isn't just based on my own experiences, but those of grieving clients I've worked with over the years.

Other Widow Rules will undoubtedly rear their heads, but for our purposes here, we'll focus on the most common and pernicious of them. That boils down to these ten:

- Do not be seen smiling. Make sure you always look sad enough.
- Don't look or act sad, especially more than two weeks after the funeral, lest this make those around you feel bad or think about death.
- No going out for anything social. You should stay home and only wear black.
- Go out and socialize so everyone knows you are okay. And for goodness's sake, don't wear anything black.
- NO DATING. Period. Ever. Or at least for six months, or a year, or several years.

113

- Date so your friends don't have to worry about you.
- Make no changes to your home involving your lost loved one until given permission by someone else. Do not remodel or get rid of any of their belongings.
- Remodel and buy some new furniture. You need a change! Also, get your late spouse's stuff out of the house so it doesn't upset people to see it.
- Don't say your loved one's name.
- Do say their name but apologize every time, because you are making others uncomfortable.

You'll notice that for each one of these rules there is a corresponding contradictory one. I really wasn't kidding about this. It is literally *impossible* to follow all of the rules, because in abiding by one, you consequently break its corresponding, opposing rule. Worse, if you try to follow these anyway, they have the potential to keep you trapped in grief indefinitely.

Recognizing that trying to follow the rules is an exercise in insane futility is the first step to finding the strength to ignore them, and to setting healthy boundaries with anyone in your life with the misguided temerity to insist that you follow any of them.

This begs an important question. Laid out side by side like this, it's pretty clear to see that these rules are nonsense. So why is that other people—especially those who have not experienced a loss like yours—feel the need to impart them to you in the form of advice, wisdom, criticism, or would-be chicken soup for the bereaved soul? Well, for starters, the Rules are rooted in a mixture of outdated cultural conventions and common hang-ups about death and loss. These conventions and hang-ups have been translated into this set of conflicting expectations people have about how we all should deal with loss. And therein lies the crux of the problem with the rules: it's easy to assume that you know what someone who is grieving needs, but the truth is that none of us are entirely alike when it comes to processing grief. That's because each person and each relationship is different. As a result, each *loss* is unique, and the person who experiences it must find their own way to process it and heal. The rules do not recognize this reality. On the contrary, their static, rigid nature flies in the face of this reality.

What is the take-away from this? Nothing you do in this period of your life is going to satisfy everyone around you. You will never be the widow they all want you to be. And you will make yourself some combination of crazy, sad, and infuriated if you try. So don't fall into this trap that so many widows who've come before you have.

Just say *no* to the rules. And say hello to Rebellious Widowhood.

The Widow's Rebellion: A New Hope

The moment you become a Rebellious Widow is the one where you decide to buck the rules and take charge of your own recovery and healing from the profound loss you've suffered. You decide for yourself what your recovery is going to look and feel like, and how you will manage the reconstruction of your life. This means being comfortable with yourself as your own driver and tour guide through what comes next. You can't afford to allow others to push you one way or another down this road.

Being a Rebellious Widow also means taking some risks. You have so much to gain, but you're going to have to stand your ground, stand up for yourself, and put yourself out there in order to seek whatever it is that you want and need to move forward. This will take courage, especially in the face of disapproval from friends and loved ones who may not understand what you're going through or how you decide to navigate your way through it.

There are those who will not understand how you can pick yourself up and find joy again. Indeed, it is very likely that there will be people in your life who feel will a righteous need to *censure* you for daring to do this. I'm telling you now that you cannot afford to listen to them. Even if they mean well, they are doing you more harm than good.

We are Rebellious Widows. We don't need hard and fast rules. These few trusty guidelines, however, will serve you well.

- Trust yourself. Grieve *your* way rather than according to someone else's wishes.
- Establish healthy boundaries with your faith, friends, and family as you navigate your loss and move forward.
- Make whatever changes you need to make to feel whole again.
- Find a way to make your cherished memories of your late partner fit into the future you are designing for yourself. Make a space for them.
- Allow yourself to find love again—if and when you are ready, and ignoring any imposed time frame.

We'll be exploring each of these tenets of Rebellious Widowhood and why they're vital to this process in the next section, and in the rest of the book as a whole. Now, I'll be up front in telling you that following these tenets is easier said than done. Right after you lose your intimate partner, you're going to be hurting something fierce. But you have to stand your ground and defend your right to whatever it is that you need right now and moving forward. Because *you* are the only person who knows what that is from moment to moment.

The risks can feel daunting. I've watched the kids of widows tell them to their face they would stop speaking them if they dated or remarried. I stood by a friend whose stated wishes to keep her recently departed husband's clothes for a while as she acclimated to his absence were totally disregarded without her knowledge. She came home from the funeral and reception to find that his clothes had already been removed and donated to charity by someone who thought they knew better.

None of this is okay. Do not let yourself be convinced otherwise.

You cannot just stand by and let people do (or keep doing) these things to you. It hinders rather than helps your healing process, and you can't afford that. What's more, you shouldn't have to. We know from research that those who take action and reorganize their lives come out healthier. Those who do not feel powerless, immobilized, and are far more likely to fall grievously ill themselves.

A Rebellious Widow makes her own decisions about what she needs to handle grief and move forward. She does not ask anyone for their opinion or permission before doing so. And she does not apologize for stating her needs and insisting that these needs be respected. If necessary, you must also be prepared and willing to put some distance between yourself and anyone who can't do this, even moving people out of your inner circle, or even your life— temporarily or permanently—if they can't get with the program.

Let's take a closer look at what it means to be a Rebellious Widow.

The Five Tenets of Rebellious Widowhood

You know by now that taking your recovery into your own hands is what is needed to truly heal. And that deciding for yourself how best to move forward into a new life of your own design and creation is a big part of that recovery. In the previous section I proposed five helpful guidelines to embrace *instead of* the widow rules. Below, let's take a closer look at these tenets of Rebellious Widowhood, so you can better understand what role each one plays in your journey.

#1: Trust Yourself to Grieve Your Way

The grief rules spring from collective so-called wisdom that has become codified into social expectations. The way these rules are invoked in your life might be what your friends and family think is best for you, or something else entirely, like an attempt to protect your late spouse's memory and place. But one of the underlying implications of the rules is that because your spouse is dead, you cannot be trusted to make your own decisions—even about how to appropriately grieve. Give yourself the time and space needed to listen to your own thoughts and feelings, and what feels right for you. Respect yourself enough to honor this. The first boundaries you will need to define and defend as a Rebellious Widow are in choosing to grieve on your own terms.

#2: Establish Healthy Boundaries

As a Rebellious Widow, you should not be expected to have time or energy for people or social structures that do not serve your ability to heal. Now is the time to take a hard look at your friends, family, and faith. These three pillars of your life should be its major supports, propping you up—not tearing you down. Are there friends and family who were not there for you, or who are being critical of your recovery process? It's okay to keep them at arm's length if they can't get with the program. Are your spiritual needs being met? Are you still comfortable in your faith, or do you need a break or a change? Do what you can to surround yourself with a healthy circle of intimates who support what you want and need to be okay. Those who are critical or controlling will hold you back as you recover if you let them.

#3: Make Changes Needed to Heal

In order to feel whole again, you're going to have to embrace change—and direct that change, rather than passively allowing it to happen. You have some time now to decide what you want your life from this point forward to feel and look like. Once you're clear on this, it's time to take stock of what needs to change in order to make it happen. Everything is on the table: people, places, interests, activities, work. If anyone questions you, play the widow card. And do so without any guilt or shame. You've already lost your spouse, something you had no say in. You get to decide what comes next.

#4: Make a Space for Your Late Partner

You're making a new life for yourself, one that is what you want and need it to be. Just because your late spouse isn't physically present anymore doesn't mean they're not a part of it. You're the one who gets to decide how to incorporate their memory into your new life. Which pictures stay up in the house or at work? How will you remember your loved one on holidays, anniversaries, and other important occasions? You're the only one who can answer these questions in the way that's right for you. You don't owe anyone an apology for how you choose to do this. Others owe you the respect to decide for yourself.

#5: Allow Yourself to Love Again

The passionate part of who we are does not die with our spouse. You—and only you—get to decide when you're ready to find love and companionship again. Other people will try to impose their own ideas about what is an appropriate time frame, but you're the only one who knows when is right for you, not to mention *who*. Finding love can mean finding romance and/or sexual intimacy again. It can also just mean finding new—or reconnecting with old—interests you love and are passionate about, and meeting new people who share your passions. Embrace life and new experiences on your own schedule, not on someone else's. Be open to letting new people and things touch your heart.

As you continue your journey through healing and reorganizing your life, keep these tenets close at hand and at heart. Revisit them as often as necessary as part of your roadmap into the future. They will never steer you wrong.

The Road Ahead

The greatest gifts of Rebellious Widowhood are healthy boundaries, the belief that you are or one day will be ready to fully experience life again, and a plan for how to get where you want to go from here. To that end, the next few chapters of this book will focus on how to:

- Prepare for needed changes
- Find, create, and seize new opportunities
- Live your life and find love again, if that is part of where you want to go

If you make mistakes along the way, it's not a sign that you ought to have listened to the naysayers. Failure is life's greatest teacher. Mistakes are how we learn. Being willing to take a chance on something that feels right means being open to finding your path forward into happiness and recovery. And you can't find a new hand to hold if you are unwilling to reach out in the first place.

Break the Rules. Make your own instead, using the tools of the Rebellious Widow to guide your way. Countering the naysayers and rulemongers will take some of your energy and courage, but it doesn't have to take it all—not if you don't let it. Set those healthy boundaries and guard them as zealously as you need to. Embrace the possibility of finding happiness again. Even if it's impossible to imagine waking up with a smile again one day, know that this is possible. It is out there waiting for you.

For now, you just have to take the next step, and then the one after that. And so on.

In the next chapter, we'll deep dive into how to decide what changes you want to make in your life and how to prepare for the new life ahead of you.

9

PREPARE FOR CHANGE

Life is uncharted territory. It reveals its
story one moment at a time.

— Leo Buscaglia

Be Prepared

I've said it before, and I'll say it again: there is a
gift unlooked for in knowing in advance that your
spouse is going to die. That gift is *time*. In the chapters leading up to this one, we've talked about how to
make the most of that time with your spouse, and
how best to adjust to the new reality you are facing as
a widow or soon-to-be widow.

But there's one thing left to do with this gift of
time. And that's to prepare yourself to reimagine and
restructure your life to be what you want and need it
to be. You'll continue the vital work that you've

already started in the days, weeks, and months after your loved one has died.

Through much trial and error, I've learned that there are three key pieces to mastering this period of self-preparation. These are to:

- Get (re-)organized
- Embrace self-care
- Lean into your support network

So why is it so important to cover these bases? Because doing so ensures your continued independence and happiness. This is not the time to allow others—even when they mean well—to determine what you need, how that should be accomplished, and on what schedule.

There is also just a lot to take care of and deal with after your spouse dies. Not just materially, but emotionally, mentally, and spiritually. You are in charge. You have to be. Because if you're not, then you're allowing other people and all that *stuff* to take charge of you instead. And that is a recipe for further misery.

When you decide to be in charge of how you will respond and adapt to this situation, you are actively deciding what needs to change (and what doesn't) to make your new life work in a way that's logical and desirable for you. How do you want employment, retirement, finances, and activities to work for you now? What makes you feel good at the end of the day? Who do you want to spend your time with? You can certainly seek advice from others in tackling some of this if you wish, but the only one who can make these decisions is *you*.

Once you have decided what you want and need to change, you'll be recovered enough to redesign your life, and to know that you are doing it your way. You'll also have reached the clarity you'll need to actually begin to go out and sculpt your new life as you emerge into it. When you open that door, you'll feel good stepping out, because everything behind you is put away neatly and can be counted on to be in place when you return.

In this chapter, we'll work on getting reorganized, and how to make that work for you. We'll also explore how to embrace self-care to be healthier and happier, in a way that fits your life. And finally, we'll cover how to reevaluate your existing support network and who belongs there, as well as how to lean in when you need them.

Let's get started.

Get (Re-)Organized

First things first: what am I talking about when I say you'll need to reorganize? Reorganize *what* exactly? Since we'll be dealing more with restructuring how we manage our health and emotional support later in this chapter, let's focus here on getting reorganized materially. That means looking at your finances, living situation, and work life. If you have kids, it also means considering how your childcare needs may be about to change.

What will need to change in these areas? Below, I've included a list of questions to ask yourself in order to determine this.

- Where is your money is going each month and what are your spending habits? Is this going to work going forward?
- Are you truly happy in your work life? Or do you often find yourself wishing you were doing another kind or work, or doing your existing work with a different team or organization?
- Is your employer supportive of your new challenges as a widow? Or do they kick up a fuss over stuff like childcare, needing sick or mental health days, or time off to manage paperwork and other stressors as a result of your partner's death?
- If you're considering a work change, how will this affect your retirement plans?
- Does home feel still like home, or do you think a change is in order? This could mean making design or remodeling changes, or simply buying new furniture. Or it could mean moving to a new home, or even a new city.
- If your partner died at home, does that impact how you feel walking in at the end of the day?

- If you are retired do you want to stay where you are? Is there some place you've found yourself wishing you could live, or a group of friends or family you want to be near?

Are there any other facets of your life that you're currently unsatisfied or unhappy with?

Even if your spouse is still alive, it's never too early to start evaluating what might need to change once they are gone. If you don't, you're only setting yourself up for exponentially more stress and heartache during what is already one of the most difficult times any of us will ever face. Fear of the unknown can be paralyzing. Mix that with fresh grief and you have a cocktail of despair in the making. Don't do that to yourself. The best path forward is to get out ahead of these changes before they ever have the chance to become yet another crisis to endure.

But that's not the only benefit to making plans for what needs to change now. In addition to reducing your stress, tackling these issues now means you'll have more time and energy to focus on what *you need* in the weeks and months to come. You'll process through your grief faster. You'll be healthier and happier.

Research shows that planning ahead now can even mean that you will live longer. Those who spend the time in the last stages of their spouse's illness preparing for their needs afterward are ready to put those plans into play as soon as the need arises. They know what their finances will be, and what changes they will need to make. They know if they will stay in their current home or will need to move sooner than later. They are prepared to get back to work or back to being invested in full-time parenting or retirement, and they know what they want that to look like.

Taking stock and reorganizing your life is the single biggest key to how well and how fast you will recover after your spouse dies. I know that the hard facts of shifting finances and living arrangements can be extraordinarily difficult to face in light of everything you'd already been coping with. It's not a comfortable process by any means. But the only way to manage this part of your coming loss is to head right into it. Have a trusted friend help if necessary. Talk to an advisor. But manage it. Don't let it manage you.

Embrace Self-Care

Now that we've hammered out how to get materially organized, let's turn to the next thing you're going to need to get back on top of: your physical and mental health. I'm going to tell you something that is less of a secret and more of an elephant in the room. Caregivers typically don't do self-care well. We focus on the people we take care of more than on ourselves. But in order to heal from the experience of losing your spouse, it's time to face that elephant and say, "Move over, Jumbo. I've got things to do."

One of those things is learning all over again how

to take care of *you*. Actively managing your health needs right now will give you a platform for a healthier outcome.

If you've been taking care of a terminally ill spouse for weeks or months, or even years, it's likely that you've let some things slide when it comes to looking after yourself. So, the first thing to do is to take stock of your health. When was the last time you had your teeth cleaned, had an eye exam, got a physical or a mammogram, or completed any other labs or tests your doctor wants done? For that matter, when was the last time you took a vitamin? You likely won't feel like doing any of these things. Do them anyway.

And this is just the basics. Next, we get to the good stuff.

When was the last time you exercised? Or took a walk outside in the sunshine? Exercise reduces stress and depression. None of this is rocket science, but it bears remembering—especially now. If you've let good habits here slide, there has never been a better time to work regular exercise back into your routine. A thirty-minute walk outside or a on a treadmill is a great start. So is going for a swim or a bike ride. Classes at the gym or your local yoga studio are another great option, because this is low-impact socializing.

A healthy diet is another simple way to take better care of yourself right now. Eating some healthy green stuff and a balance of nutrients makes us think and feel better. Grievers tend to crave comfort food, which typically means carbs with a side of carbs. While you might feel better indulging in the short-term (and honestly, no judgment here, do what you need to do while you're really in it), eating your feelings is not a great long-term strategy for healthy living. If you like to cook—or even if you'd just like to learn to be better at it—cooking a healthy and tasty meal just for yourself can be an extraordinary act of self-kindness. There are hundreds of free websites with simple, healthy, flavorful recipes available at the touch of a button. Use those resources. Try sourcing ingredients at a farmer's market if there's one in your area—you can usually get a good deal, and you can't beat the quality or freshness of the produce you'll find there. If all of that is too much, order some make-it-yourself kits online, and have a week's worth of meals delivered to your doorstep. That way you get the satisfaction of really creating something good for yourself, and you don't have to face going to a grocery store.

Getting plenty of sleep is more important now than ever. Grief causes exhaustion, which reduces our motivation to exercise. That said, sleep can be hard to come by now, especially in the initial days and weeks after a death. It's pretty common to wake up around two in the morning with insomnia during this time. To help get your sleeping schedule back to normal, I recommend the following helpful tips:

- No screen time (phones, tablets,

computers, TV) for one hour before
bedtime

- Try to empty your mind by journaling before bed, even if it's just to make a list of what you need to do tomorrow
- Make sure your bedroom is a comfortable place to sleep—adjust bedding, lighting, and the temperature as needed
- Exercise daily
- Avoid caffeine later in the day or evening
- If needed, try relaxing herbal teas or ask your doctor what supplements are safe for you
- If you are really struggling, there are also prescription sleep aids that can help

Finally, tending to your emotional health is vital right now too. You don't have to be strong all the time. Cry when you need to, even if it makes others uncomfortable. If you have hobbies, now is a terrific time to throw yourself back into them. Do the things that bring you joy. And when you can, smile. Laugh. Enjoy happy moments whenever possible. And if anyone dares offer a negative opinion about that? As a wise woman once said, ain't nobody got time for that.

Take good care of yourself. You deserve it. And it's what your spouse would want for you too. As long as you're adopting healthy habits, it's okay to put your own spin on them. Do it your way.

When it comes down to it, healthy boundaries are

the ultimate form of self-care. Let's take a closer look at why this is.

Lean into Your Support Network

The final key piece of reorganizing to recover is recognizing who your people are at this point. Who is still in your life who has stood by you? Who has supported you rather than questioning and criticizing your decisions during your spouse's illness and death process? I blogged throughout my experience both times I was in the process of becoming widowed and, looking back, it was easy to see who was there and who disappeared. Some were loudly critical as they walked away from my new life. Others simply vanished.

When it came to those who were critical of me and what I knew I needed then, I realized something important. Allowing that critical, judgmental energy to remain in my life was hampering my ability to recover. They were distracting me from my path and soaking up massive amounts of energy I did not have to spare. So, I told them to shape up or ship out. Others I quietly distanced myself from. And still others decided to support me despite being confused and somewhat mystified by my choices at the time. Those are the people with whom I now have a stronger bond than ever.

Once I knew who my support network would be, I could seek them out to safely talk out my plans. I had people I could call to cry with or celebrate happy moments—mine and theirs—without making them feel weird that *the widow* was there. Or worse, in my case, the *double widow*.

The bottom line is that not having a support system isolates you. It makes you vulnerable to ruminating on your thoughts and your self-doubts about the difficult decisions you've been having to make. Even if you are more of an introvert, you still need a support system to get through this time. Having these people in your life will keep you healthier both physically and emotionally.

Make Your List

So where do you find your support network? We're going to do an exercise here. I want you to make a list of everyone in your life who you currently count on for any kind of emotional or other caring support. This list might include family members, friends, faith-based friends if you attend a house of worship, online contacts, close professional colleagues, neighbors, and perhaps a therapist if you see one. If you attend a support group of any kind, or if you're part of a community related to your passions or hobbies, people from there might go on this list too. If you're writing this list out by hand, leave a good amount of space between the names.

For the first part of our exercise, next to each name on the list, I want you to add at least a few words to describe the kind of support that person gives you. For someone you became close to from a faith-based group, for instance, you might write "shares and supports my values" or "offers good spiritual guidance." For a therapist, you might put "sound professional advice" and/or "listens confidentially and without bias or judgment."

Other types of support might include:

- Emotional: This could mean someone who will listen and hold space for you when you simply need someone to be there. Or it could be someone who offers loving touch —pats on the back, long hugs, holding you when you need to cry. It can also mean someone who can and will make you laugh when you've had enough of crying.
- Informational: Someone who is a well of trustworthy knowledge or who can help point you to other useful resources.
- Organizational: A person who can help you untangle your thoughts and apply them to your current moment. Or who can help you physically get organized if your home, office, schedule, or paperwork are a mess.
- Domestic: Someone who supports you by providing meals, doing chores or errands,
- Encouragement: Who are your cheerleaders? Who are the folks who say "I believe in you" when you need to hear it?

It's also worth noting down who is empathetic or

sympathetic, as well as who praises, reassures, encourages, or affirms you and your experience, and who expresses concern about how you're doing.

Now onto the second part of our exercise. This time, we're going to go through our list again and write down who does the *opposite* of all the things you've just noted above.

Who is critical, judgmental, or tells you that they disapprove of how you're handling your grief process? Who doesn't want to listen to the ideas you have for what you might want moving forward? In other words, who is causing you extra heartache right now and making you expend extra energy explaining or defending yourself? Who is making your life more difficult than it has to be in an already difficult time?

Write this down too. And as you review your list after you've done this, it's time for the third and final step of this exercise: evaluating how much each person is giving and taking, and literally crossing people off the list of who you receive emotional support from right now if they either aren't giving anything or are taking too much.

Now is not the time to worry about spending your energy trying to fix these relationships. These folks may return to your inner circle over time, or they may not. Bottom line: they are not your responsibility. If you have doubts, ask yourself this very loaded question: Would your late partner approve of their words, how they are acting toward you, and the impact they are having on your recovery?

If someone you are leaning into for support tells

you your plans are wrong, your ideas are misplaced, or that they want you to say or do things differently, then they are not good for you right now, plain and simple. Even if you truly believe their intentions are good, their behavior is *not*. It doesn't matter who this person was to you in your previous life. If they do not support or fit what needs to happen right now, let them slide back from being friends to just acquaintances, at least for a time. If it feels scary to set permanent limits on these relationships, plan to invite them back in at a closer level of intimacy after you are firmly headed where you want to go.

By the same token, look to your completed list for the people you now know you *can* count on to support you. This list is your team roster. Use it!

Online contacts and programs can also provide support from a safe distance if that is where you are at emotionally. It's a great way to set firm limits and have a relationship you do not have to commit to. Support groups can be amazing if they are healthy and will empower you to make your own plans, rather than holding you to theirs.

Choose Your Own Adventure—and Adventuring Companions

You are facing a challenge that can be scary. But it can also be liberating.

Life moves so fast, and we're all so busy in this digital age. Sometimes we end up just falling in socially with whoever chooses to be in our lives. Or we end up allowing ourselves to get stuck with the people we meet at work, church, or local activities, instead of consciously and deliberately choosing who is in our lives. How often do we really get to stop and say "Wait! I am deciding what happens now. And I am deciding who is a part of that and how."

Over time, our support systems tend to create themselves rather than the other way around. We make room for those who are amazing and add immense value and enrichment to our lives, yes. But all too often we also make room—and allowances— for those whose energy is negative and stressful, but for whom we feel a weird sense of responsibility to keep in our lives.

To be clear, I'm not advocating cutting multiple people out from your world forever in a cruel way. But I am suggesting—strongly—that reorganizing for your recovery is easier and healthier when you surround yourself with and lean into those who share your desire to reimagine your life. Communicate what you need to those around you clearly and firmly. Kindly is good, too. But stand your ground.

You need people around you now who can be excited—genuinely—for the changes you need to make after your spouse's life has ended. There are those who will feel, for their own reasons, *threatened* by these changes instead. Giving your time and energy to those people right now is going to hurt more than help you.

If you learn how to create strong, healthy boundaries in who gets to be in your support system and who doesn't now, it's a skill that will serve you well not just now–but for the rest of your life.

Next up, we'll take a closer look at how to create and embrace new opportunities coming your way, and how to take the first steps on the road to the new life ahead of you.

10

ENVISION A NEW LIFE

> I learned to love the journey, not the
> destination. I learned that it is not a
> dress rehearsal, and that today is the only
> guarantee you get.
>
> — ANNA QUINDLEN

A Path Forward

Not a one of us asked to be a widow. But now that widowhood has arrived, the only way through is to embrace change and figure out how to make your new life work for you. First, though, you have to figure out what those changes will be. This means actively envisioning your new life and what you want it to look like. What do you want *yourself* to look like so that you'll be able to thrive from here on out? How do you see yourself and your life a year from now? Five years from now? How do you want this time to unfold?

If you can transition into allowing yourself to think about your life without your spouse, and what that life might offer, you will be on your way to taking charge of your new world. You will have the deciding vote about where you are going, how to get there, and how you will live. The alternative is deciding not to think this through and getting stuck in your grief because you haven't given yourself a path out of it. If this happens, you risk never truly healing from your loss. Instead of embarking upon a new journey and a new life, you'll be left holding onto the remnants of what came before, only without your spouse. This path leads to bitterness and unhappiness.

On the other hand, if you allow yourself to see what you want your new future to look like and get ready for it, you'll give yourself the tools you need to shift your mental state from grief and pain into discovery and joy. You are not leaving your spouse behind. You are taking the love they gave and the things you learned from your life together, and using all of that to forge a new life of your own.

In this chapter I will be challenging you to let yourself imagine what dreams you might have once had, but did not get to pursue, as well as any new dreams that may be surfacing now. We'll also cover how to get clear on exactly what it is you want through techniques like making vision boards (not as hokey as it sounds, I promise). Finally, we'll take a hard look at where you're currently spending your time and energy to reevaluate where you want to allocate these resources going forward.

Now is the time to listen to yourself. What is it you want for your future? It's time to make it yours.

A Time to Dream

You have been facing this unwanted new future for a while now. You knew your spouse was terminally ill, and you have already begun reorganizing the parts of your life you knew would have to change—finances, living situation, work or childcare needs. Now it's time to think about more than just the necessities. What is it that you actually *want* now? These past weeks and months when you needed a distraction, what did you dream about doing in the future to get you through the hardest days? What thoughts, desires, or flights of fancy have continued or now started to bring you ease and joy?

This is a time of sadness and grief, yes. But it's also a time of unexpected freedom. When we marry, we give up some of our independence and, often, some of the dreams we had when we were on our own. Some of your plans, however unrealistic they may have been, went by the wayside. Now you have more life experience under your belt. You might just be in a place where you can put those dreams into play if they still have a hold on your heart. What dreams have you set aside that you can dust off and look at in a new light at this stage in your life? And what new dreams have you picked up along the way—or are only just starting to percolate now?

These dreams—new or old—can be anything from a career change, moving residences or cities, picking up new interests or hobbies, or simply dropping old interests or hobbies that never really fit you to free up more time and space to find new ones. And here's something you may not have considered: Rebellious Widows have one tremendous advantage when it comes deciding on a major change in course.

That's right. You can play the widow card. People who know you've suffered such an immense loss will have a harder time telling you 'no' when you go after what you truly want in life now.

If you have already taken charge and drawn healthy boundaries around what you need (as we've discussed in previous chapters), fewer people in your circle will doubt or question you. So, what are the ideas, images, and fond hopes that cross your daydreams? Can you afford a shift toward them? Can you make them happen in a way that makes sense for you financially and emotionally? It's great to be able to bounce ideas back forth about your dreams with your support team. Just remember that when it comes to making any decisions, you hold the only vote that counts.

The Dream I Dreamed

As I write this, I'm sitting in my private practice office. Before Linda's death I would have been in a county building, sitting at a cubicle in a windowless cavern. I had colleagues I enjoyed working with and a great career. I also had to be at work at seven in the morning and was dealing with high stress and furlough days, because the recession was in full tilt. When Casper died, I was on the road with hospice daily, doing another job I absolutely loved, but I drove in excess of 100-150 miles a day in traffic. I was also dealing with an administration that created more stress rather than reducing it.

Now I am in an office I designed, looking out a window at a view filled with treetops, with my Oodles (of poodles) at my feet. I see clients who seek me out for my expertise, and I get to travel to speak at conferences nationwide teaching how to cope with grief and loss and dementia. I have time to write and publish books that matter to me because they make a difference.

My new dream provides for me and my family, sets an example for my adult children, and allows for the resources needed for time away with my wife. It wasn't easy to get here. It involved me digging deep to put in enough hours to make the business successful with my business partner. It's meant a lot of appearances to build my reputation as a speaker and surmounting a learning curve to manage social media. And you know what? It has been totally worth it.

If you have unfulfilled dreams, big or small, whether they still call to you from long ago or are brand new, take a moment to stop and look, listen. Now is your moment. Whether it's the dream of more income, the need for your time to be structured, or setting a goal simply to have one at this time, look at anything and everything that you even *might* want to do with your life right now and in the near future. Make your list.

What can provide for your needs at a cost that will not sabotage your recovery? What dreams will fit who you will be in your reorganized life? If you need to, consult someone in whatever field your dream is seeding itself in. Research it. Evaluate it. But give each idea a chance, even the ones that might seem crazy. Maybe you are retired and want to volunteer, but in something completely new. Had Linda lived we would be living in Florida again, and she would be a volunteer at Homosassa Springs State Wildlife Park, feeding manatees and sharing her love of Florida's critters and waterways. Is relocating to your dream place on the table? Maybe there are friends or grandkids you want to spend more time with now. Is that feasible for you? There will never be a better time than now to shift priorities and refocus on what matters most to you now, whatever that may be.

This is your time. Use it wisely. Figure out which dream you want to harness and ride to wherever it is you want to go from here.

Create a Vision Board

Of all the tools out there to help you envision something you want for yourself, nothing I've seen works better than creating a vision board. If you're not familiar with this technique, it's literally what it sounds like: a visual collection of images and/or words that illustrate what your dream looks, smells, tastes, sounds and feels like. Usually a vision board takes the form of a collage, either physically on paper or cardboard, or through a digital platform like a Pinterest board.

Vision boards allow us to put our dreams in front of ourselves daily. What's more, they allow us to transform those dreams into *goals* that we start to believe are possible and stay motivated to achieve. They do this in part by forcing us to name what we want and acknowledge out loud to ourselves *that this is where we are going*. Research shows that those who create a vision board and keep it somewhere they can see it every day really do reach that goal more often than those who simply think about it. (This is part of why Pinterest is so popular.) Once your vision board is complete and visible, you will find yourself reviewing your progress toward your goals and working toward them. Why? Because you can *see* it. Your dream, your goal is staring you in the face every day.

Currently, mine always include the beach, because it is my happy place. The part of my dream I'm still working to achieve is a home near the beach with a small space for groups and retreats, a garden with fruit trees and frangipani, and a view of the sunset. When I look at my board, I can hear the waves and the seagulls, feel the sand, and smell the salt air. Seeing these images front and center where I work each day helps me stay motivated to keep checking off boxes for each stepping stone that will make achieving my dream possible.

When you're ready to make your own board, first decide if you want to make a physical board or a digital one. I'm a tactile and visual person, so I prefer physically making one. Hunting through magazines for pictures to cut out and paste in is a fun part of that process for me. If you're going to make a digital one, there are programs or platforms you can use online. Pinterest is easy and free to use. The only word of caution I'll offer if you're using a digital board is to make sure you keep an image of it or a link to it some place where it's visible so that you'll remember to look at it every day, like your device's desktop background or as a browser bookmark. Remember: vision boards work better the more time you spend looking at them.

Here are a few tips to observe while making and working with your vision board:

- Assemble your pictures in any way you want. This is your reorganization, after all. There are no rules here. (Surprising no one, I love that part.)
- Be sure to include anything that will say to you, "This is where I'm going."
- If it feels right, include a picture of your spouse. It's okay to take them with you in spirit.
- Decorate! For my physical boards, I like to

use glitter glue and word stickers intended
for scrapbooks. You can hit a craft store
for those if you like.

- Display it. If it's a physical board, put it
where you will see it when you wake up, or
where you spend the bulk of your time
during the day. Your dreams and goals are
not up for debate, so make sure you are
not inviting criticism by placing it where
doubters will spot it, unless you are
prepared to shut them down.
- Look at it. Focus on it. Your board is
there to remind you of the promise
you're making to yourself to achieve your
dream and what lies ahead when you
reach it.

One last thing to note: your vision board can
evolve with your dreams and goals. They are a great
tool to use to check-in and assess not just your
progress, but also whether your goal needs to be
updated or adjusted from time to time. Your vision
board is there to remind you of your dreams on tough
days, and to celebrate your progress as you achieve
the milestones—large or small—that will create your
new life.

Look at your board. Dream about it. Focus on it
before bed to shape your thoughts while you sleep.
And *always* remember that your spouse would not
want your life to stop because theirs did. This board

is a tool you can use to make your world complete again, in a new way.

In addition to looking ahead to how we want to spend our days in the future, this is also exactly the right time to reevaluate how you're living your life right now.

Reorganize How You Spend Your Energy

In grief we lose energy and stamina. We lose our ability to concentrate, and to focus. This makes it incredibly difficult to keep up with all the things we used to put our energy into. There just isn't enough of you to go around right now to fulfill all your previous obligations. That's why it's important to figure out where and how you want to invest your energy now and in the future, and to reorganize things to fit your new set of priorities.

Now is the time to look at how much you are doing, where and for whom, and if each of those expenditures is really necessary or worth it. Trying to continue to manage everyone else's needs at this time in your life without assessing how much you can reasonably do is an act of self-harm. It sets you up for exhaustion and a sense of urgency that will never let up for you—when you are already running low on resources. It also creates unrealistic expectations for those around you.

It doesn't have to be like this. You can find a sense of mastery and control over your new life. You just have to be willing to set realistic limits and determine where you are willing to invest yourself now. Rather than racing around trying to keep up, you can say no. You can do less. You can even do *more* in areas that fit your new priorities.

To assess where your time and energy are going right now, I want you to make a list. (Yes, another one!) This list is going to be broken up into a couple of different sections and there are going to be two columns for each section.

The three sections of the list (which we'll explore separately in three subsections below) are:

- Professional life
- Relationships
- Interests

And the two columns that will run through all three sections are:

- Left side: Current expenditures
- Right side: Possible changes

Give yourself plenty of space in the right-side column for notes. We're going to build this list, piece by piece, going through the rest of this chapter.

This exercise can be a real eye-opener. One useful technique is think of your time and energy as a limited form of currency, where there is only so much you have to spend each day. Once you see a physical list of all ways in which you're trying to spend such a limited resource, you might be surprised (or even taken aback) at how much you're trying to do.

Work

Let's look at work and career first. This is an area that frequently shifts after a spouse dies, both in focus and in energy investment. It may even shift prior to their death as you struggle to balance the demands of work and caregiving. For widows of working age there is almost a reckoning after the funeral is over. When your spouse is dead, you may find yourself reflecting on how much your work really, truly mattered when you look back at your life together as a couple. Not just your income, mind, but the work itself.

For the left side of our list, let's look at your current expenditures:

- How many hours per week and per day are you spending actively working at a job or to support your career? Include any hours spent at volunteer positions.
- How many hours per week and per day are currently devoted to school or training (including ongoing professional development) to support your career?
- How much time are you spending each week or month on other work-related activities, like research, networking, or travel? And how much does all of that

extra work cost you, in both time and
money?

- What about time needed to decompress
after a workday or week? Include this too.

And now for the right column. How do we evaluate how you might want to invest yourself professionally from here on out? Here are some things to
consider adding to this side of the list:

- If you've recently gone back to work full-
or part-time, do you find yourself feeling as
invested in your work as you did
previously? Is your job paying what you
need now that your household is relying on
one income if before there were two?
- Do you need more education to advance
your career and/or your income? If so, how
can you make that happen?
- Think about your workplace and the other
people in it. Is this really where you want
to be?
- Are your current colleagues the people you
want to spend your days with and invest
your time and energy into? If they are
amazing and supportive, maybe the answer
is yes. If not, this is something to really
consider.
- If this is not where you want to be, what
could change? Location? Your agency or

company or district? Your specific assignment?

- Maybe it's time to consider a new career altogether. What could that be? It has to support you, provide security, and bring you more energy than what your current career brings to the table. You want to leave at the end of the day or night feeling good about your choice and your place in the greater scheme of things. What might that look like?
- Alternately, maybe it's time to look at retirement. How could you make that happen, if not now then sooner than later?
- If you are already retired are you doing things in your retirement that you feel good about? Are you getting the energy you put into your activities back out of them again, or do they leave you feeling drained and dissatisfied?

Work is not supposed to consume us. Yes, we need to put our best effort in. We need to strive for our best. But no one wants to spend every day in a place where we walk out exhausted, don't want to even show up to, or where our colleagues are unpleasant to deal with. This can be your opportunity to recreate this part of your life. Trust me, few people will argue if you say you simply cannot stay because your loss has really changed who you are and how you want to live your life.

Relationships

Relationships and how they evolve (or don't) are a big part of the grief process and your recovery and reorganization. The reality is that some relationships become tenuous while we are deeply involved in caregiving for a spouse with a terminal illness or recovering from grief. This process and the experiences you've been through change a person. It changes how we view life and our relationships with other people. And it may require us to temporarily withdraw from some of the people in our lives because we simply don't have the time or energy for everyone and everything right now.

Now is the time to evaluate the status of your relationship with the people who were in your life before all of this happened, and the people who are in it now.

For the left-side column, consider these key points for each person you are currently giving time and energy to, or who you gave of yourself to before your spouse fell ill. Again, give yourself some room to work here. You may end up with little clusters of information for each person listed here. That's great!

- Who is in your life right now or was before your spouse got sick? If it helps, you can break this list down into subcategories:
- Family
- Close friends and extended family / Support network

- Friends
- Colleagues, teams, and team members
- For each person on this list, how much energy are you investing to keep this relationship functioning smoothly?
- How much energy and support does this person give back to you?

And now for the right column. Things to consider here:

- For each relationship that you listed in the left column, look at how much energy you are giving them and how much you're getting in return. Does the give and take of energy in this relationship feel balanced right now, or is it lopsided? Relationships with children and other dependents are going to be lopsided, with you giving more than you receive, generally. But your other relationships, if they are healthy ones, should be at least fairly balanced.
- If a relationship is out of balance, who is the person giving more to it right now? If that person is you, is what you get from this relationship worth continuing to put forth more energy than the other person is giving? If not, is it worth having a frank discussion with this person about what you need from them?
- If the person giving more energy is the

other person, why is that? Why can't (or won't) you put in at the same level? Is this relationship crowding you with too much attention or too many expectations? Is this one you may have outgrown? If so, it's okay to redefine it, or to simply let it go.

While you're evaluating each person listed on the left side, also consider who you've become closer to than you were before your spouse got sick. And who you are less close to.

- Who came and helped when you needed it?
- Who did you think you could count on for help but might have let you down?
- Who are you now reluctant to call for support or to share a moment?
- Who offers you unconditional support and care?
- Is there anything you're not currently getting from this relationship that you wish you were? Or vice versa, something you would like to be able to give that you aren't currently?

Thinking through these questions can point to how relationships have already started to change and evolve. Recognizing this now can help you decide what you want from each relationship moving forward. Needs shift. Priorities shift. We change in ways we never imagined possible. And sometime that means we outgrow some relationships and grow *into* new ones. This is a natural part of life.

Even so, this is a painful process for most. Give yourself permission to back off and give relationships that aren't working time and space to figure themselves out. (That means that, at least for the time being, the other person does the work, not you.) The same goes for family relationships. Some will swing into an inner circle, and some will head for the outer bands. It is not necessary for you to make all of them work. Your energy should go to those in your inner circle, where the energy exchanged is reciprocal. Over time, some of the more distant folks may shift back. Some may slip away completely. If this person wants to be there for you and with you, they will figure it out. You can't make them do this. You shouldn't have to.

Interests

In this final section of our energy expenditures list, there are a few more areas to tackle outside of professional concerns and our relationships with other people. And that's our relationship with ourselves and our stuff: our interests, hobbies, and belongings. Yes, believe it or not, everything you own is something you have energy ties to.

For the left column, let's look at where your energy is currently being spent when it comes to your personal interests, and how this has worked for you in the past.

- What hobbies or activities do you pursue now, or did you previously pursue before your spouse became ill?
- How much time and energy do you (or did you) spend on these activities?
- How much energy and enjoyment did you get back from each of these activities?
- What things do you own or have in your life that take up your time, energy, or other resources like money? Or even that just take up space in your home. This could be anything from an extra car or motorcycle sitting in the garage, to items in a storage space, to a cabin in the mountains.
- Note how you feel when you walk into each room or outdoor area in your current living space. Pick a particular room. Stand in it. Does this room evoke positive feelings or negative ones? Or both? Try to describe how each room makes you feel. Is there something specific about it or in it that makes you feel that way?

And now it's time for the right-hand column. What could stand to change for each thing you've written on the left side?

- If you've determined that one of your

existing hobbies or interests might not be something you want to do anymore, is there a new activity you might want to try instead? Or something you used to do a long time ago that you'd like to get back into?

- Alternately, there may be something you've already been investing some time and energy in that you want *more* of now. How can you shift priorities around to make more time and energy for this now?

- If you've identified any possessions that take up a lot of time, energy or space in your life or your home, are they worth it? Is it time to simplify or downsize? This is a great time for that.

- Remember: when it comes to getting rid of your *spouse's* stuff, the schedule is entirely up to you. Be cautious about getting rid of things too quickly. If having their belongings in the house is painful, box them up and put them in storage for now. If your spouse left instructions about who was to receive things, follow through. Do not allow anyone else to do this for you. It is part of the healing process.

- If you've identified things about your home or specific parts of it (a room, the garage, your yard or outdoor living space) that you're not terribly happy with, it might also be a good time to put your

energy into some renovations or
redecoration.

- Do you hate the color of a room? Are the
couches too much of a reminder of
something, or not your taste for your new
life? It's amazing how much even a small
change in décor can improve how you feel
about where you live.

Changes in your personal life can be reinvigo-
rating but take some energy to put into action. They
can also cause the most internal and external conflict
for you. Evaluate carefully, move deliberately, and do
this your way and on your schedule. Be honest. And
when it comes to trying new interests, remember you
can always change your mind and try something else.
This is your new life. *You* get to decide how to
spend it.

What You Make of It

Your new life will emerge from your careful evaluation of the current state of your life, and your reorganization of it based on the new set of priorities you
set for yourself. This process is bound to include
some fun discoveries. Be open to them when they
arise, and remember that nothing is set in stone. You
can always make changes along the way. You can add
people back in, change the colors of your walls, and
even change where the walls are.

The way forward will be cobbled together from a

combination of old plans, new dreams, and your goals and passions. Once you have your roadmap in place, your sense of self will shift into a new you, a reinvigorated you. You can and should use the tools and skills you've gained here to make this happen.

A Rebellious Widow gets to determine her own path and who is on it with her. This may also include adding in a special someone to join you. In the next chapter, we'll look at when might be the right time to love again.

11

LIVE YOUR LIFE AND FIND LOVE AGAIN

> It is so easy to waste our lives: our days, our hours, our minutes. It is so easy to take for granted the color of the azaleas, the sheen of the limestone on Fifth Avenue, the color of our kids' eyes, the way the melody in a symphony rises and falls and disappears and rises again. It is so easy to exist instead of live.
>
> — Anna Quindlen

Give Yourself Permission

At this point, you've assembled the tools and skills you need to reorganize and take charge of your life. You understand the mindset you'll need to cultivate to move through grief as you contemplate the paths that lay open to you now. You are becoming a new you. But there's one step along your journey to Rebellious Widowhood that I've saved for last. And that is embracing your need for love and intimacy, for a life that will eventually include someone new.

If you've read other grief books, you may have noticed by now that very few of them attempt to tackle this topic. It's controversial. It's uncomfortable. But this is a natural and important part of life that there is no reason to shut yourself off from forever if it's something you still want.

As with everything in grief reorganization, each step of your healing process must be allowed to fall into place in its own time—meaning on *your* time, and on your own terms. There is never a guarantee in life of meeting someone you're crazy about even once, let alone multiple times. But one thing is certain: if you don't even open yourself up to the possibility, that door will stay closed.

Give yourself permission to allow a new love to enter your life. You can do this while holding your late spouse in your heart, in a place that is reserved for them alone. Despite what some people will say, these two things are by no means mutually exclusive. You are not replacing your late spouse. You are adding new love to the love they left with you.

This chapter will prepare you to include a new love in your recovery plan. We'll cover how to make room for this, as well how to actually incorporate a new special someone into your life. Finally, I'll give you some tools to help you face down any critics who feel entitled to judge you for your courage to love again.

But how will you know when you're really ready?

Preparing to Love Again

If I had to boil down all the best advice I can give you about finding love again as a widow into a single bit of wisdom, it is this: give yourself as much or as little time as you need. The tricky part here is *figuring out* how much time you need, so let's zero in on how to do this.

Like many challenging phases in life, this one should begin with a frank self-inventory of where you're at emotionally. The first thing to ask yourself is whether you are truly done with your relationship with your late spouse. Have you said all that needs saying? Are there any resentments tied to this relationship that you still need to work through?

The best tool I've ever found for this part of the process is journaling. It doesn't matter if you do this in a physical bound journal, on loose sheets of paper, or using a word processor. Just write from the heart. In the act of writing about your feelings, you are implicitly giving yourself permission to have and to *feel* them, whatever they are. And by naming them, you're giving yourself space to heal. Any conversations you need to have with your late spouse can easily take the form of a letter written to them. Say what you need to say. And what you do with that letter (or letters) once you've written it all down is up to you. Keep them, delete them, or even burn them if it feels right.

Once you finish processing through this on paper, you'll find you are far more ready to think about the possibility of a new love. This is a timely bit of progress, because it's time to start figuring out what you want your love life to look like moving forward. Once again, journaling about this is a great way to explore and organize your thoughts.

First, how do you feel about the idea of emotional and physical intimacy with a new person? For most of us, our feelings here are bound to be complex, to say the least. That's okay. Give yourself time to work through whatever comes up, and practice self-compassion. It's okay to be scared. It's not easy to make yourself vulnerable to someone new. But you already know how rewarding it is when you find someone you care about who is worthy of that trust.

It's also important to think through what you're looking for in a partner. What standards will you hold this person to, in terms of their character, values, and behavior? Are you looking for someone who is optimistic, has a good sense of humor, or who shares your passion for a particular hobby or topic? Write that down! What are your deal breakers? What kind of life do you envision living with someone new? What does being loved mean to you? What does it look like?

It's okay to use the rich history you had with your late spouse to set priorities for who will accompany you into your new life, so long as you remember that you are not looking for a clone. You are looking for someone who fits you and your life as it is now.

Trust your instincts. They've brought you this far. Once you feel the time is right and you have a fair idea of what you're looking for (and *not* looking for), it's time to make plans to set your new love life in motion.

Finding Love... How Exactly?

It's one thing to know what you want and to reach a place where you're ready to start looking. Actually *finding* someone to embark on a new relationship with, though, can feel daunting—especially if it's been years, or even decades, since you last hit the dating scene.

There are a few things that I and my clients have found helpful at this stage. For starters, if you have single friends in one of your close circles (friends, family, and support system), or even among old friends you have not talked to in quite some time, now is a good time to get their insights as you contemplate moving forward. Single friends who have experienced the loss of a spouse can be an especially helpful resource. Regardless of whether or not your single friends are widowed, never underestimate the power of a good wingperson. If nothing else, they will be an amazing morale booster or cheerleader during this new period of exploration.

Dating apps are also an option. Because new ones pop up like wildflowers, I'm not going to recommend specific ones here. Rather, I suggest you join a healthy widow group on social media to see what other people are using and listen to or read up on which ones other people like. Word of mouth can tell you which apps are popular and good, and which have lousy reputations.

Your existing social circle can also be a great resource to tap—but only if they know you're looking, as some might be hesitant to mention someone they want to set you up with unless you've communicated that you're ready. Many of the widows I work with find that dating another widow or widower is also an attractive option, particularly old friends with whom there may have once been a spark. As always, if folks in your social circle can support you in your reorganization and allow you to enjoy being in the arms of someone new, wonderful. If they can't... well, we've already talked at length about the importance of healthy boundaries.

Once you start meeting people and getting to know them, I recommend that you continue journaling throughout this part of the process. Evaluate how being around a new dating or relationship partner makes you feel. Does the way they treat you affect you positively or negatively, or both? If something feels wrong, again, listen to your instincts.

Finding someone to experience love with again is one thing, but it's another to begin to integrate that person into your life. Next up: a crash course in doing just that.

Incorporating a New Love

Introducing a new love after the loss of your spouse is not easy. That said, it doesn't have to be emotionally charged or scary. You are not a seventeen-year-old asking to go to prom. You're an adult, and you have a new life ahead of you after pulling through one of the most devastating periods of your life.

Once you're ready to introduce your new love to the important people in your life, however, there is a way to go about it that will help you minimize the potential for hurt feelings or damaging relationships on all sides. Like many conversations in life, it just needs to be handled with thought and care.

To this end, we'll focus on the two biggest potential hurdles here: how to talk to your loved ones about your new relationship, and how to incorporate your new partner into holidays and other important family events. By the time we're done, you'll feel confident when it comes time to start this conversation with the people who love you.

How to Talk to Your Loved Ones

The hardest part of coming out as a Rebellious Widow who has chosen to love again is telling the family. It's an odd space to occupy. You are an adult. You have been married. You are not having an affair.

And yet it feels much like you are when you try to tell those closest to you that you have found love again. They are the ones who were also closest to your late spouse, and loyalty after someone dies is a powerful thing.

The sad part is that you are not being disloyal, but your desire for love will be viewed through that filter by many people. Even so, you have to tell them, and you have to do so in such a way that you're not implying an apology, or that you're offering them a vote on how you ought to live your life. If you come at the conversation in either of these two ways, you risk handing too much power over to others about how much their opinion counts in the decisions you must make about your own life. And if that happens, your new love may never be accepted.

The first thing to do when preparing to tell your circle about your new love—once you're serious about them and vice versa—is to temper your own expectations. Don't expect your friends and family to be wildly enthusiastic. We're just shooting for acceptance here. Remember that others may not yet have come to terms with this loss as quickly as you have, especially if you did much of your grieving up front during a long illness.

The order in which you tell people also matters. If you have adult or older children, they should be among the first you talk to. Younger children, on the other hand, should not be made aware of a new relationship until you are certain your new partner is likely to be a permanent fixture in your life, and then only slowly. Since some kids mature faster than others, there is no magic number for when kids are old enough to be told sooner than later. If teens know you miss having a partner, they may be more open to a new one if you reassure them that their parent is not being replaced. Small kids naturally attach names and titles to people they see as filling a role in their family, so your new love will have a significant chance of being given some kind of title similar to your late spouse once they become a known entity. Obviously, that's a big deal for everyone involved and should never be undertaken lightly. Until such a time as you and your new partner are ready to take that plunge, visits between you should take place away from your home and without your children's knowledge.

In addition to older or adult children, a close friend or two are good candidates for being among the first people told—in part so they can support you through telling everyone else. For this reason, pick whoever is the most likely to be nonjudgmental and supportive among those you are closest to. You know by now who your cheerleaders are. Once you've told the kids and your close support system friends, you'll be ready to tell family and the rest of your close circle, and then anyone else who should know.

A final word of advice: don't be afraid to practice these talks or to at least come into them prepared with a set of talking points. Those close friends you tell first? If they're willing, get them to help you practice for any potentially difficult conversations coming up.

Holidays and Family Traditions

Holidays and special family traditions have included your late spouse since you became a couple. You are now facing birthdays, graduations, new babies, weddings, funerals, and holidays with someone new. This can be tricky.

The best advice I have for you here is to find ways to honor the place of your late spouse, but not at the expense of your new love. When we blend families that include people who have died, we have to make the one we lost part of our new life. They are present at the dinner table. They are with us at weddings, when we open holiday gifts, when we barbeque on the 4th of July. Everyone there is acutely aware that someone is missing and someone is new.

Do everyone a favor and just talk about it—and don't wait until that big day to start the conversation, because that can put undue pressure on everyone. Instead, break the ice ahead of time, and include your new love in these conversations. Discuss plans early, clearly, and openly with them and with your family. Include your kids in the conversation, if you have kids.

During these discussions, allow everyone to share their thoughts and feelings, including any feelings about the person you have lost. Let everyone weigh in on how they'd like to honor your lost loved one while still making room for joy on special days. Maintaining an open, honest, and compassionate line of communication about how best to do this will help you to avoid damaging important relationships, because this allows everyone to feel loved, heard, and respected.

As plans develop, make space for changes in other family members' plans as they adapt and make space in return. Give yourself and others permission to slow down, do less, and to change plans if it becomes too much. Be sure you and your new love have an agreement to this effect. And remember, if you start to feel a strong sense of *this is not how it used to be*, that is because it can't be how it used to be. And that's okay. You are doing the best you can under painful circumstances, and you deserve to be happy here, today.

Don't push yourself too hard on that first holiday. If you do this right, you will begin making joyful new memories while keeping the one you miss present on important occasions. And that's the goal here.

How to Withstand Criticism

No matter how well prepared you are going into introducing a new love to your circles, you will encounter criticism for daring to love again as a widow. Remember those widow rules we tossed out a few chapters back? They will rear their ugly heads. It's better to accept now that this is going to happen so you can prepare yourself for it.

You are about to find yourself in the unenviable position of having to stave off some very strong opinions and so-called best wisdom of the ages. Even if you feel well-prepared, it's likely to catch you off guard at times. You will be surprised at who can't seem to finish processing their own grief from such a distance. Remember, if they are still stuck in grief over your spouse, they will assume *you* are too. Any move toward a new relationship is going to set these folks off. This group may include other widows who have decided to stay in mourning status indefinitely. You have to be ready to face critics, both for your own sake and that of your new relationship. This has the potential to make your new partner feel insecure and unwanted. It can cause real pain for both of you.

So, what is the best way to prepare for this? Just like we did with our introduction conversations, we're going to practice. This is an exercise you can do in the privacy of your own home, alone and in front of a mirror. Or if you like, you can ask a close friend to roleplay it with you to practice in a "live" setting.

And the first thing to master? Ah, yes. A time-honored tradition. The 'I really cannot believe you just said that to me' look. You might be surprised, but this is one of the best weapons in any Rebellious Widow's arsenal. Silence is powerful. And a well-timed glare paired with a moment of stunned silence can really get the point across. It also gives the speaker a chance to pause, realize they've said something rude or presumptuous (probably both), and to apologize if they've got the good sense and grace to do so.

If they do, great! If they don't, you can absolutely choose not to respond *at all* to what they just said. In fact, if you want, skip the glare and just walk away.

They'll get the picture. You don't have to engage with people about this unless you want to, and unless you feel up to it. If you need to, you can always take a step away and come back to that conversation when you're calmer.

If you do choose to verbally rebut criticism you receive on the spot, it's best to interject it as soon as possible. Don't let them get going on a tirade. Interrupt firmly but calmly, if you can remain calm, and just say, "I'm glad you have concern for me, and I am sure you know that I do not take my future lightly. I hope you will be one of the people I can count on to welcome [your new love]. If you can't I will be sad, but I'll respect your decision to step away until you can."

Alternately, you can try something along the lines of, "I am certain you have a reason to believe you know what is best for me in recovering from the loss of my spouse, but I am the one actually going through that loss. And I am making decisions that fit my needs. I appreciate your concern."

Practice these responses until you know them by heart. They're not easy words to say, but you will be better for saying them when you need to. And know that not every response you get will be critical. Make space for others to offer their approval, support, or congratulations. If you hear remarks that include "but," "maybe," "have you considered...," "how can you know?", "isn't this too soon?", head them off at the pass.

If you prepare yourself and remember that you

deserve to live a happy and full life, to be loved, you can stand strong in the face of people who just can't resist giving you their unasked for opinion. We are Rebellious Widows, and that's how we roll.

The Courage to Love

Moving from reorganizing your life to finding new love is complicated and exciting. It can also be awkward and a bit bewildering. And you have to do it in full view of folks who will make it known that they have an opinion about it all. But now you have a toolkit for how to approach this exciting new phrase using healthy boundaries and communication to keep you, your loved ones, and your new relationship healthy and safe.

Be aware of your new partner's needs and how much of an impact the criticism you two receive is having on them. And be firm when it comes time to decide who should remain close in your life, and who has earned themselves a demotion to a more distant social circle.

Most of all, own your new life and your new love. You have worked hard for it. You've walked through fire to get here. Be proud of yourself for that and protect every bit of that joy you've seized that came your way.

Know that you deserve to love and be loved again, regardless of what anyone else has to say about it.

In the following final chapter, I offer some parting wisdom and advice, and some words of inspiration to take with you as you take the next steps of your journey out of grief into healing and joy.

12

A LIFE ON YOUR OWN TERMS

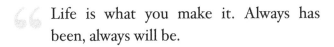 Life is what you make it. Always has been, always will be.

— Eleanor Roosevelt

The Picture of Grief—A Portrait of Illusion

Historically, the images we have of Queen Victoria stand as the classic "perfect" example of widowhood: frozen forever in grief. She never remarried, and only ever appeared in portraits and photographs in dark clothes, seemingly in perpetual mourning. Back then, there were no visible photos that depicted her enjoying her life after her husband's death. Not only did she follow the widow rules—I genuinely think they may have been modeled after her.

I did not want to be *that* widow. The one who lived for being a widow, who defined herself by her loss.

But here's something I learned along the way that I found affirming. Even Queen Victoria, the poster child for the widow rules, broke them. There is some evidence that she did find love again. According to stories and some surviving historical records, Victoria went on to secretly marry her groom, John Brown. Her children had brought him on to work at her estate on the Isle of Wight, thinking that being led around on her pony might bring her some joy after Albert's death. Boy did it. Their romance ensued, and the relationship was disapproved of in the family, by her staff, and even in some papers. Her second marriage, however, remained secret, revealed only in gossip secondhand and later upon her death.

And after John died? She found love still again with Abdul Karim—though it remains unclear whether their love was romantic or not. What is clear is that the two were lovingly devoted to one another. Their relationship was the subject of the 2017 film *Victoria and Abdul*, starring Dame Judi Dench.

Even the queen of England felt that she had to hide the fact that she broke the widow rules from her family, her staff, and her nation. That's how strong a hold these rules have on us—but only if we let them.

Jill the Rebellious Widow

It was February of 2010, and Linda had been terminally ill for four years. We'd finally called hospice in.
My wife was dying.

The doorbell rang and I answered, laying eyes on
the butchest butch nurse I had ever seen, dressed all
in black.

"Hey, I'm Casper," she said. "It's the man in
black's birthday."

"What?" I asked, ever articulate.

"Johnny Cash," she said in her Southern drawl,
stepping into our home and our hearts as I let her in
the door.

Casper went on to become one of Linda's closest
friends in the time she had remaining, during which
Casper took care of her like family. They had everything in common, spoke the same language: nurses,
southern, same generation, lesbians.

I will be forever grateful for the close bond they
developed. It took the fear from Linda in our nightly
talks when she couldn't sleep. She had someone new
to laugh with, to call her out on her crap when she
didn't want to take her meds. Their friendship gave
her peace and made her feel better about leaving her
family behind.

And, as it turns out, even while dying, Linda had
designs on my heart. She informed me that after she
was gone, I should marry Casper. The kicker: she
wasn't kidding. I wasn't ready to hear this at the time,

but much to my chagrin, once I *was* ready, I realized she was right.

Not long after Linda passed, I found comfort and love again in Casper's strong arms. Linda and I'd had decades together. Casper and I only got three and a half precious years before she too became gravely ill. Once more I became a caregiver. And once more, I lost the person I loved and with whom I'd started rebuilding my life.

But I will always remember Casper and the magic of falling in love again, at a time when I needed so dearly to remember what it was to be *alive*. Those eyes. That smile. The happiness we found, despite everything else going on.

Suddenly I was a fifty-year-old double widow, who could not drive for a time and walked with a cane due to the lasting impact of a stroke. My kids were adults. One of them was getting married, with a grandbaby on the way. I was starting the second half of my life, but on my third lifetime.

Once more, the widow rules reared their ugly heads. Once more, I rebelled.

And in walked Stacie. Somebody probably should have warned her. I sure didn't!

There is something incredibly special about recovering from the loss of your second wife with a woman who knew *both* of your wives and could still make you smile. Stacie talked me through my bad dreams and found funny moments or things to do to bring some life back into my world. She showed me kindness where I had learned to steel myself. A mortician by trade, my grief did not scare her. She could—and still does—hold my hand and listen to me talk about what I've lost without flinching or shying away from it. She also challenged me to deal with it head on. Her kindness and willingness to see the good in people has helped turn around some of the jaded parts that grow from the rule enforcers trying to help determine your future. Stacie's support has strengthened me in making this new version of Jill the Grieftalker, speaker, educator and author the best version of who I want to be and where I want to be. (I am certain Linda and Casper have been cheering her on from the other side. They had plans for me as well. It kind of feels like a committee on Zoom sometimes).

We didn't sneak around for long, even when we were still trying to figure things out. I was over the need to defend my choices by this point. When we were ready, we had a tiny, unannounced service with just close family and a few friends. Once again, some refused to attend.

Has it been perfect?

Are you kidding? Our life is a constant whirlwind. I'm learning to take time out to experience new places. Stacie is learning what it means to have daughters, after not having kids and being single for more than a decade. I had to learn how *not* to be a caregiver. After so many years of needing to make everything all right and manage so much, relinquishing control was a huge learning curve. I think everyone—myself included—breathed a sigh of relief when we got past the first three years and settled in.

We've found new experiences – New Mexico for the International Folk Art Festival. Seattle and Duck Tours with my cousin and her son. The Central California Coast. Laguna arts events. Laughlin. Vegas. Louisiana. San Francisco. Alaska. The Caribbean was supposed to happen, until Covid-19. When I travel for speaking engagements and conferences, Stacie comes with me most of the time, giving us time together and me an organizer, cheerleader, and coordinator. The second half of our lives will be our chance to explore the world while being grateful for being together and still here. During the Covid pandemic, she has helped me organize a home studio where I can see clients online, teach classes, and do podcasts and videos. Our two grandsons and our dogs, the "Oodles," bring a great deal of joy to our lives.

Have I stopped missing Linda and Casper? Not a chance. It hurts sometimes, but the grief is over. They are with me, and I have learned to temper how often I mention them to ensure I respect Stacie's role in the present. I'm glad for each of the lives I lived with my wives. I'm grateful and happy with the one I have grown into now, and the woman who has become my partner in it.

I'm still here. I laugh and love and hurt and breathe, then laugh some more. I am living proof that you can get through this—that you can recover and know joy on the other side. I want others to know they can too.

You don't need my permission. But you absolutely have it, and I have your back.

The Next Step Down Your Path

You have been working so hard to reorganize and reshape your life, to make of *the now* something that fits the way you want to live and love from here on out. You have the tools, mindset and healthy boundaries you need to succeed. Now is the time to walk your path as a Rebellious Widow.

But what does that life actually look like?

The trappings of that life are your own to decide, but every Rebellious Widow's path shares some of the same steps.

Step one? *Ownership.* Specifically, *your* ownership of your own life and experiences, your own decisions and choices. You may have had help from your support system along the way in figuring things out. Even so, you made the important decisions about how to walk your path through grief, finding closure in your relationship with your late spouse. You chose for yourself what you wanted on the other side of that loss and how to achieve it. You know that grief is not forever, that you can and will and *have* healed.

Step two? *Self-confidence.* You now know that you possess the strength, resilience, and courage to face life's greatest challenges and come out stronger on the other side. You have asserted your independence, not just from the widow rules, but from any people in your life who mistakenly think they have the right to dictate what your emotions or choices should be because of your loss. You've established healthy boundaries to make sure that others don't infringe on the space you're creating to explore new opportunities and new joys. That means that some relationships and friendships may have taken a backseat, while others have come to the forefront. You've made your peace with that.

Step three? *Self-compassion*. You have learned to be patient and kind with yourself. After having lived through such a profound loss, you know better than to sweat the small stuff. You've also learned to trust your sense of what's right for you, and to give yourself the time, space, and self-care you need to be exactly the person you want to be, to have the life that you've dreamed of. It's okay to focus on taking care of *yourself* when you need to. You deserve it. And if and when you decide it's something you want and are ready to explore, you know that you deserve to love and be loved again.

You have a plan now—a goal for what you want to achieve for yourself. You're owning it. You know you can do it. And you know who in your life has got your back when you need support and encouragement along the way.

You, Rebellious Widow, are going to be more than okay. You're going to be amazing.

Welcome to the Good Part

We Rebellious Widows are a unique bunch with amazing energy, and I love keeping in touch with my fellow travelers on this path. Once you fully embrace your new identity, it's time to make it your own. I want to hear about your journey!

Books can reach a wider audience, but speaking to groups in person and online in forums, in classes I teach, and on podcasts and live streams is the best part of my new life, and the best way to connect with me. My speaking engagements take me to community events and conferences across the country and around the world. I speak on grief, loss, dementia, and living a bold new life. I also speak for professional groups, educating therapists and others about how to use the new grief recovery paradigm I have taught you here. You can find my upcoming speaking dates on my website, www.jilljohnsonyoung.com.

I am also on every form of social media that this middle-aged Rebellious Widow can manage (with some help from a talented college student). You can find me on Facebook, Instagram (https://www.instagram.com/jilljohnsonyounglcsw/), Pinterest (https://www.pinterest.com/Grieftalker/), and Twitter (@ jilljohnsonyou1). Podcasts and links to interviews are also available on my Facebook pages for Your Path Through Grief (https://www.facebook.com/yourpaththroughgrief/) and Jill Johnson-Young, LCSW (https://www.facebook.com/grieftalker/), as well as a page for a weekly grief chat I do with Debra

Joy Hart, who also lives to find the joy and growth that grief can offer (https://www.facebook.com/fridaygriefchat/). You can join our talks weekly on Fridays and send us topics to discuss. Videos can be found on my You Tube channel as well as my website. Finally, I can be reached via email on my website contact pages. I really do respond!

ADDITIONAL INFORMATION

If you're looking for further resources on healing from grief and loss, I authored a grief workbook, Your Own Path through Grief: A Workbook for Your Journey to Recovery, as well a few books for children on these topics. I'm also working on a forthcoming second grief workbook for adolescents. My books can be found on Amazon and through my website

And finally, I am licensed in California to work with clients as a therapist. If you're not local to my area, I've also been working on building a referral network based on personal recommendations from trusted colleagues in the field. If you reach out to me via my website, I can provide that list for you should you need it.

My Wish for You

Do something for me.

One last time, close your eyes and sit in the quiet. Be still. Listen to the sound of your breath and the slow beat of your heart.

You are still here.

Your spouse loved you. So much.

You did all you could.

You will never, ever forget them.

You are the expert on what is best and right for you.

You are allowed to smile, to laugh, to feel the sun on your skin. Put your toes in the water. Relax. You deserve to feel joy, to get excited, to make plans.

Live your life.

It's yours. So, go on and take it. Chin up. Shoulders back. Eyes forward.

I wish you peace, happiness, and ever so much love.

Always and always, may you find love.

ACKNOWLEDGEMENTS

When you lose two wives with three kids, remarry twice, change careers, and recreate your life there are a lot of people involved, and family takes on a whole new meaning. A lot more deserve recognition, but I'm told I write too much, so I did my best to leave it short. If I left anyone out, I will take the blame. Each and every person who has touched me as I became the Rebellious Widow should know I am grateful to you.

My childhood to menopause girlfriends group, thanks for always being there, especially Wendy Marshall, who laughed while we learned how to empty catheter bags, and Hai-Ping Hwang Twigg, who brought the laughter. To my Tribe, thank you for the love and support for Linda, Council meetings, and for the times you were there during all of this. My family- mom, aunts, cousins, sisters- your support and your twisted senses of humor made it all doable.

My Casper and Young family- your love and keeping this rebellious widow in the family folds mean more than you know. My team at CCS, especially my business partner Sherry Shockey-Pope, my absences are in this book. I appreciate your understanding. My hospice teams of the past- your lessons and your support made living with dying so much easier. You know I think the world of you.

The writing here has had so many edits, yet it is all mine and my vision, and for that I owe Julia Watson a tremendous debt. She took 250 plus pages of good intention and challenged me to make it meaningful and helpful. Mission Accomplished.

Thanks as well to Adam Davis, an inspirational speaker and author who took the final manuscript and said it was a much needed resource for so many- and then took it over the finish line to you, the reader.

Those in the Parkinson's, Lewy Body, Dementia and Pulmonary Fibrosis communities online and in person, you make living with these diseases possible and provide a safe place to vent at 2am for those still in the trenches. Thank you. You are a lifeline of humor, coping and making do. And you get falling, potty issues, and the jokes (and occasionally colorful language) necessary to get through it all.

Jo Muirhead and Nicola Kick Morris, thanks for getting me from an ethereal idea to here. Jo, your coaching has challenged me, and Nicola your cheerleading and permission to be outrageous is appreciated. Thanks as well to the work group under Jo's direction that has inspired, challenged, and supported this process, and all of my aspirations to make a difference.

And finally, to the grievers I have worked with in hospice in two states over two decades, and the countless clients, and email contacts, conference attendees and folks who reach out in so many ways- I hope this will speak your experience, and honor your process. We only thrive as well as the people with whom we surround ourselves. You are why I do what I do.

NOTES

3. Your New Role as a Caregiver

1. Richard Schultz and Scott Beach, *Journal of the American Medical Association*, Dec. 15, 1999, vol. 282, no 23, p. 2215-2219.

CPSIA information can be obtained
at www.ICGtesting.com
Printed in the USA
LVHW041934131222
735156LV00014B/478